MYSTERIES
OF GEORGIA'S MILITARY BASES

-
- GHOSTS
- UFOS
- & BIGFOOT
-

JIM MILES

Schiffer Publishing Ltd

4880 Lower Valley Road • Atglen, PA 19310

D1066789

Other Schiffer Books on Related Subjects:

Georgia Spirits and Specters. Beth Dolgner. ISBN: 978-0-7643-3256-2

Spirits of Georgia's Southern Crescent. Christina A. Barber. ISBN: 978-0-7643-2945-6

Haunted History: Atlanta and North Georgia. Corinna Underwood. ISBN: 978-0-7643-2854-1

Haunted Northwest Georgia: The Legend of the Ghost Hearse and Other Spooky Tales. Beth Youngblood. ISBN: 978-0-7643-5214-0

Designed by Justin Watkinson

Type set in Digital/Univers LT Std/Minion Pro

ISBN: 978-0-7643-5355-0
Printed in China

Published by Schiffer Publishing, Ltd.
4880 Lower Valley Road
Atglen, PA 19310
Phone: (610) 593-1777; Fax: (610) 593-2002
E-mail: Info@schifferbooks.com
Web: www.schifferbooks.com

For our complete selection of fine books on this and related subjects, please visit our website at www.schifferbooks.com. You may also write for a free catalog.

Schiffer Publishing's titles are available at special discounts for bulk purchases for sales promotions or premiums. Special editions, including personalized covers, corporate imprints, and excerpts, can be created in large quantities for special needs. For more information, contact the publisher.

We are always looking for people to write books on new and related subjects. If you have an idea for a book, please contact us at proposals@schifferbooks.com.

To **Earline,**
for everything.

CONTENTS

ACKNOWLEDGMENTS

I would like to thank the following for generously allowing
me to use material from their extensive websites:

Robert Lautner of Ghosts of America (www.ghostsofamerica.com)

Caroline Curtis of Bigfoot Field Researchers Organization (www.bfro.net)

Peter Davenport of National UFO Reporting Center (www.ufocenter.com)

Fort Benning has trained hundreds of thousands of soldiers since World War I. This statue at the National Infantry Museum and Soldier Center honors their service.

INTRODUCTION

So, why are military installations so paranormally active?
I believe it is a function of the nature of military affairs
and the nature of the various phenomenon.

Ghosts

Military bases are haunted because of the makeup of those stationed there and the military profession itself. The military exists to keep America safe. Unfortunately, occasionally wars and other types of conflict have to be conducted. Fighting involves death, painful wounds, and permanent injuries. Military personnel leave their bases and sometimes do not return. The survivors are scarred by their losses and memories.

Even in peacetime, the military is a dangerous profession. Men and women die in training. Their job requires the use of dangerous weapons and massive machinery, their activities often undertaken when they are exhausted, or operating in dangerous terrain, often at night. Soldiers hurl themselves out of airplanes, and there are maneuvers and live fire exercises. Such a level of death, danger, and loss, concentrated in relatively small communities, will result in supernatural manifestations.

And then there are the civilians. Most soldiers, airmen, and seamen, are painfully young, often away from home for the first time. There are missed births, birthdays, anniversaries, and holidays, and anxiety for those abroad. Their anguish is palpable.

Perhaps the souls of those who died overseas search installations seeking loved ones or the last place where they knew peace.

It should not be difficult to believe that military bases can be haunted.

UFOs

Georgia has some of the country's most important military posts, including air force bases that handle America's latest advanced aircraft, infantry, and armor bases where armies are trained to maneuver and fight, a submarine base with half a dozen nuclear submarines whose mission is to unleash hell on the cusp of Armageddon, and one of the nation's most important electronic surveillance facilities. If UFOs are alien craft or host earthly enemies, these are places that would naturally attract their attention.

Bigfoot

We have military bases larger than counties and containing vast areas of swamps, forest, and river valleys—prime habitat for a secretive species. Bigfoot activity is rampant at three of our army installations.

001

DOBBINS AIR RESERVE BASE

Dobbins, now surrounded by the city of Marietta, located twenty miles north of Atlanta, was established in 1942. Two years later, the Bell Aircraft Company built an adjacent factory, which constructed 668 B-29 Superfortresses during World War II. Postwar, Dobbins has hosted units of the Air Force Reserve, Georgia Air National Guard, and a variety of aircraft. Bell, which constructed 394 B-47 Stratojets, evolved into Lockheed-Martin, which has produced C-130 Hercules for half a century and constructs the modern F-22 Raptor and F-35 Joint Strike Fighter. The base trains crews for the C-130 and stands ready to deploy forces worldwide.

Dobbins is an urban military base, part of Metropolitan Atlanta, yet still part of the old South. As such, its most prominent paranormal phenomenon consists of ghosts.

Building 452

Building 452 was constructed in the 1960s as a base housing unit, but in 2000, it reopened with classrooms and offices for air conditioning, heating, and utilities instruction. Master Sergeant Jeff Welch, a Water Fuel System Management supervisor and instructor, worked in the building for ten years. After only a few weeks he heard unexplainable noises and experienced strange events.

"It's constant," he told Senior Airman Christian Bozeman, 94th Airlift Wing Public Affairs, for an article, "Ghostly Encounters on Dobbins," published on October 14, 2011. "You never know what will trigger it."

The belief is that a child died in the house, suffering considerable pain, and its ghost remains trapped there.

"When it's very quiet and still, you can hear it best. Some of the growls are long and low."

The "haint," which is what Welch calls it, is even willing to work nights. "There are times when the doors will be opened and the chairs turned around. Even the blinds will be drawn all the way up on occasion, and they are always kept down."

Once a co-worker thought Welsh had called out to him, "Come back," but Welch had said nothing, and no one else was in the structure.

The entity roams the hallways and pulls some of its pranks there. The building is kept at seventy-two degrees, but sometimes the hall directly outside Welch's office will be much colder.

"As soon as you cross the threshold," he said, "the temperature is drastically different."

Some might attribute such a thing to an erratic thermostat, but that doesn't work in this instance.

"We're utilities, so we know about A/C and the ducts in the house," said Master Sergeant Marc Mood, utilities instructor, who shared an office with Welch for two and a half years.

Mood does not believe in ghosts, but he knows what he hears. "Even when there is no wind, I hear sounds like somebody is wailing or whistling. I hear it all the time."

Welch is more open to supernatural occurrences now, saying he is "not a person that's skeptical, and I do believe there are spirits here still."

Happy Together Forever

The antebellum Gardner House was used for many years as the officer's club for Dobbins Air Force Base. The house was constructed around 1850 and in 1863 was sold with 225 acres to Josiah Sibley. It remained in the family until 1940 when the government obtained considerable land for construction of the base. Mrs. M. S. J. Sibley was one of 140 displaced families, and her home was one of only five not demolished. It was utilized as guest quarters for government officials and visiting dignitaries and as a club.

Cashier Geneva Perry worked there in 1984 when she had an impressive encounter. She was there alone in the building one wet Saturday afternoon when she heard the front door open and close. Knowing she had the only key, Perry was alarmed and went to see who had entered. She found no one. After resuming her work, she heard footsteps behind her and turned, she told Diane R. Stepp of *The Atlanta Journal Constitution* for the October 31, 1985, issue.

> "I was upstairs in the office; I heard the sound of shuffling feet and the rustling and swishing of taffeta-like skirts. I turned and looked at the door and there stood the vision of two slightly built elderly people—a man and a woman. She had on a long skirt and the gentleman had on just plain overalls. They were just standing there

looking at me." The ghosts said nothing, but moved toward her, coming "so close to me that my ears actually burned." After several minutes passed, "I felt a hand touch my arm, like to say goodbye." The couple turned around and exited through the door. "They never looked back."

On several occasions while she worked at the club alone, Perry would see both apparitions in the lobby or on the stairs. Their presence was accompanied by a scent, "a distinct odor—sort of old, musty, spicy-pleasant—that was not there when they were not there."

Perry had the impression they "were the servants to the owners of the plantation at the time Sherman was on his way south. They hid and more than likely died in their hiding place. But no one knew that, and so they were never buried."

Although Bobbie Jackson, a past club manager, did not believe in ghosts, he "cannot explain what happened" during Christmas of 1977. He had locked up one night and gone home, only to return after midnight to retrieve some keys. He found a light on that he knew he had turned off earlier.

"As I ascended the stairs to my office," he told Stepp , "I felt as if I was walking in a cloud of steam and detected a very putrid odor." Only seconds later lights in the party room began blinking on and off.

"I don't believe in ghosts," one-time manager Joe Goss told the *Marietta Daily Journal* on October 29, 1984, "but I know there's something in there. One day when I was supposedly alone, I heard footsteps walking across the floor above me. I ran upstairs to see who was there, but there was no one. I swear I'll never go back in there alone again."

One time air force security officers Art Cleveland and Earl Martin had the responsibility of checking the building after closing hours in the mid-1980s.

"The house is unbelievable," said Cleveland. "Lights we know we turned off when we left the club would be on again when we passed by on rounds."

"Once, I drove by and saw an upstairs window, that I knew to be nailed shut, open," Martin said of his odd experiences at the house. "The light was on in the room when I got upstairs but there was no one present. To make things worse, I couldn't even close the window by myself."

Additional reported phenomenon included self-flushing toilets and shifting furniture.

Although a number of homes survived destruction during the Civil War, a typical tale alleges that the Gardner House was spared because an Englishman living there had flown a British flag, making Sherman believe it belonged to a foreign national.

As to the identity of the ghosts, some claim it is the English owner, who committed suicide and has since made common cause with other spirits, while others attribute the activity to the two servants who somehow were buried alive while in hiding.

UFOs

On July 21, 1952, an unidentified object was registered on the radar at Dobbins. The commander of the base reported that it was at an altitude of 50,000 feet and zipping along at 1,200 miles an hour.

On March 10, 2000, at about 1 a.m., a man was parked across the street from Dobbins, "to watch the jets make their midnight runs," he informed the National UFO Reporting Center (NUFORC). After a while he decided to sit on the hood for a better view. He saw a Lockheed C-5 Galaxy cargo jet land, which was a normal event, but a few minutes later, when several helicopters also landed, his curiosity was piqued.

"There's a lot of fuss over that C-5," he thought. "I wonder what's up with that."

He walked across the street for a closer look, and after half an hour, the plane stopped on a runway beside a hanger. He then "noticed guys in what looked like light gray army fatigues run around the plane and hangar." He found that odd, it being an air force base.

The men worked to unload a cargo draped in a tarp from the big plane. A hard wind caught the edge of the tarp and "lifted just enough for me to see a round-shaped craft that seemed to glisten in the hangar lights almost like it had a slight glow."

The soldiers quickly caught the tarp and covered the craft, moving it into the hangar. The witness complained, "Nobody believes me; they say you saw a jet, but I know what I saw, and that was no jet."

Paranoid and Delusional

Those on the outer edge of reality propose, according to Mr. X, that there is "a major Bavarian Illuminati facility . . . occupied by the cult of the serpent (human and alien collaborators)," which is slated to be "the New World Order regional control, and for continued 'Montauk' or 'Phoenix' Project operations." The claim is that Atlanta will be a "FEMA regional center, which is appropriately placed since Atlanta is to become a capital within the NWO (New World Order) redrawing of boundaries."

Richard Sauder (*Underground Bases and Tunnels*), says an "underground Pentagon facility" lies beneath Kennesaw Mountain, a Civil War landmark. It will be used "as a 'defense' installation for the surrounding thirteen states."

The webblog *METAFILTER* (metafilter.com) claims Dobbins is a "test site for plasma and anti-gravity air craft, experimental crafts, and weapons." He exhibits a sad case of rampant regionalism, fearing such activities being carried out by "good ol' boys (and girls)."

002

FORT BENNING AND LAWSON ARMY AIRFIELD

Fort Benning, established in 1917, is proudly called the Home of the Infantry, training hundreds of thousands of Americans for the US Army in every conflict since World War I, and hosting many active duty units ready to deploy around the world when called upon.

Many leaders, including Dwight D. Eisenhower, George Marshall, Omar Bradley, George Patton, and Colin Powell served, or were trained here, on a campus of 287 square miles.

Fort Benning has 35,000 military and civilian jobs and supports 120,000 active duty and civilian employees, their dependents, reserves, and military retirees.

The National Infantry Museum and Soldier Center, located at Fort Benning, is a $100-million-dollar, 190,000 square-foot facility that explores the history of the United States Army from the Revolution to Iraq with dioramas, exhibits, and films. A World War II company area has been preserved.

Ghosts of soldiers past are encountered in army barracks at Fort Benning. This World War II complex is preserved at the National Infantry Museum and Soldier Center.

Ghosts

Fort Benning has an extraordinary number of hauntings. The witnesses to this ghostly phenomenon are primarily women and their children, left home while husbands and fathers are at early morning Physical Training (PT), working, or deployed overseas. The men are typically skeptical when their spouses report supernatural phenomenon, at least until something strange actually happens to *them*. Often these trained, battle-hardened warriors are more freaked out than their wives, which leaves the women smugly satisfied.

Almost every haunting involves opening and shutting doors, followed by not just footfalls, but heavy, boot-thudding steps. Perhaps soldiers are returning home in this manner because they could not come home from overseas battlefields in life. A number of old soldiers still seem to be marching through residences across Fort Benning.

Most of these spirits appear to be soldiers from different eras who were once stationed at Fort Benning, but there are also ghosts of former residents of the land, including Native Americans, farmers, , and slaves.

Fort Benning's ghosts are active and persistent, plaguing family after family over the course of decades, which has caused some to dread being stationed at Benning, particularly if they had been stationed there in the past.

Civilians, women, and children are home far more often than active duty army personnel. As mentioned, ghosts often manifest themselves while the soldier in the family is absent. In some cases, the ghosts cease all activity when the husband and father returns following lengthy deployments to troubled areas around the globe.

Spooks generally give new residents a grace period of quiet before they start their repertoire.

All this paranormal activity at Fort Benning makes you wonder if lots of people live in a few haunted residences, because people so frequently move out of them, or is the whole damn base infested with spirits?

In October 2000, Deannah, her soldier husband, and their two small children moved into housing on Arrowhead Road in Custer Estates, she informed *Your Ghost Stories* (yourghoststories.com) in 2009 in a story titled "Soldier's Home." As she lived there with the children, she noticed "a few strange happenings," not scary so much as annoying. A toy airplane powered by batteries activated itself, while the TV would shut down. The clothes dryer door once opened independently [my kids thought that was cool]. Things were misplaced. Her husband attempted to explain each event, and she waited for him to experience something odd.

When her in-laws visited, she and her husband went shopping and returned with new baking sheets, which were laid atop the oven while all sat in the living room awaiting their takeout dinner.

"All of a sudden, it sounded as if those baking sheets hit the floor; it scared all of us," Deannah said. She and her mother-in-law rushed in to see what happened, "and the sheets were still on the oven." Everything else was also in place.

The husband had shrugged off the lightweight phenomena he had witnessed until one day, in May 2002, when they were sleeping late. He "and I were lying in bed and were awakened to the sound of our wooden screen door opening, the front door being unlocked, closed, the chain put on, and then the footsteps on the old hardwood floors (combat boots make a distinct sound when walking on old hardwood floors) that went all the way down the hall and stopped in front of our bedroom door."

She turned over to face her husband, his "wide eyes and laying there stiff as a board." He whispered to her, "What's happening?" She reminded him that strange things occurred in the house.

They waited fifteen minutes, but nothing else happened. The husband got up to search the house and found nothing amiss.

"I don't think I've ever seen him as scared as he was that morning," she said. "He doesn't even like to talk about it to this day. It made a believer out of him."

On another *Your Ghost Stories* entry, Soldier I described a bizarre situation on November 17, 2009. When he visited the on-base home of another soldier in his company, he was met outside by a third comrade, "who told me that this home was haunted and not to speak a word of it inside."

Upon moving in, the occupants had immediately noticed eerie events in the house, "like things missing, movements out of the corners of their eyes, doors slamming and flying open." When the soldier called his mother to describe these incidents, things "got worse."

One night the soldier saw someone pass through a room. Thinking it was his wife, he got up to see if she needed his help. He saw a woman in the kitchen wearing a red dress, but it wasn't his wife. He found her upstairs, terrified and standing against a wall.

"She told him there was a man in ACUs (army combat uniform) in their bedroom, that she thought it was him, and when she tried to embrace him, he was gone," said the soldier.

At this point, the soldier went to retrieve his weapon from a spare room, "and all the other doors in the home flew open and, just as quickly, slammed shut."

Next he spotted a dark figure slip into a bedroom occupied by their sleeping infant boy. When the door refused to open, the man kicked it in as the figure passed him exiting the room. He found his son "had a cut from his ear to the corner of his mouth."

A soldier of Native American heritage was summoned to perform a "spiritual cleansing," involving "sage and oak leaves while praying and hanging pictures of Jesus." This soldier said, "there was evil unrest in their home and the (ghostly) woman of the home wanted harm done to them, but the father and children were at peace."

About a week later, the Fort Benning housing office told them of a tragedy that had occurred in the house. "The husband returned home from deployment to find his wife having an affair and his children calling the lover Daddy." He gathered his family in the kitchen where "he shot them and killed himself."

This monument honors soldiers who served in World War II, Korea, Vietnam, and the Global War on Terror. National Infantry Museum and Soldier Center.

Around ten years ago, Olepapajoe moved into a base house constructed about 1934, "a two-floor, three-bedroom, and three baths in a stucco structure." Only air conditioning and gas heating had been added, and the structure had "a lot of creaks and noise," he wrote *Your Ghost Stories* in 2011.

With Olepapajoe were his wife, two-year-old son, and a four-year-old daughter. Two other daughters were away at college.

One summer, his wife and younger children traveled to Kansas to spend time with her father. Around 10:30 one evening Olepapajoe was downstairs watching TV, when "I heard what appeared to be someone walking down the stairs." He muted the TV and listened. Hearing the steps again, he went to the stairs, saw nothing, then searched downstairs and upstairs, finding nothing and seeing that all the locks were secured. He returned to the living room, and, hearing the steps again, raced to the stairs to again see nothing. He often heard the steps, but thankfully not every night.

Two days later, Olepapajoe was asleep at 2 a.m. when, "I felt a strong pressure on my back as I lay on my stomach. I woke up and tried to get up but couldn't move."

It felt like two hands were holding him down. Fully awake, he was unable to move, although he tried strenuously. He thought an intruder was assaulting him, but even though he could move his head about, the soldier neither saw nor heard anything. After several minutes the pressure ended, leaving him "terribly frightened." He concluded that a spirit "didn't like me being in the master bedroom."

Olepapajoe was spiritually prepared the next night, reading Psalms from the Bible aloud and reciting the Lord's Prayer in every room in the house, a practice he repeated each night. It worked, for those "footsteps stopped and I no longer had any hands pushing me into the bed. All seemed to be well."

Olepapajoe told no one of these experiences. Later, when one daughter came home from Florida State University for a visit, she slept in a small guest room. After the first night she asked her dad, "if I heard or felt anything strange in the house."

"No," he replied. "Why do you ask?"

As she had prepared for bed, "she felt as though someone was in the room looking at her." After she laid down, the "big heavy solid wood door" opened very slowly. She thought a parent was checking on her, but saw nothing, and then she "felt someone sit on the bed" beside her. She dove beneath the covers, "said the Lord's Prayer and asked for God's protection," and would not leave the bed until daylight. Olepapajoe asked her to tell no one else the story.

When the younger daughter was eight, she "told me that in the master bedroom back at Fort Benning, she saw a dark figure that pushed her into the curtains." She never again ventured into that room by herself.

In the bedroom she shared with her younger sibling, "she would see figures, mostly women wearing . . . 'old time clothes.'" They never harmed anyone, "but just looked at her and her baby brother."

When Olepapajoe finally told these stories to his wife, she said "that she too felt 'creepy' in the house and hated living there," but didn't want to alarm him.

THIS GHOST DOES TOILETS

On *Your Ghost Stories*, GuySoldier1 laconically reported his experiences at Fort Benning. In December 2009, he was trying to sleep in the bedroom upstairs, but he "kept hearing the sound of the loose spring in my chair popping" downstairs. He debated checking it out, but as he looked at the doorway, he kept "seeing a dark half silhouette" in the door frame.

Waking early for PT, he found the foot rest of his recliner pulled out and the television activated. The previous evening the leg rest had been in and the TV off. While dressing he heard the ice maker, which had stopped working two days earlier, dropping ice, but when he checked, there was no ice.

"On many occasions my wife will ask why I sprayed so much cleaner into the bathtub and toilet." He had never cleaned the toilet. "She'll come down to ask me this with all this excitement on her face that I finally cleaned the latrines, just to be disappointed by my honest denial."

When she returned upstairs, the toilet was "all scrubbed out and rinsed, but dry."

He thought that if his mother-in-law were dead, she would clean the toilet, "but she's still going."

He felt his residence was "a little on the unrested side."

One active duty soldier wrote of experiences that he and his runner had at the building where they worked nights. He conducted some Fort Benning paranormal research online and found the descriptions of others to be "spot on—boot steps walking down the halls, doors opening and closing." They had thoroughly searched the building on a number of occasions, "and have yet to see anything or find any explanation . . . We have both felt like we have been watched constantly." He was saddened to hear "of the suffering of families in their homes here on Benning. However, I'm happy I'm not just hearing things."

A soldier named Kirkland often visited a friend who lived in Indianhead, and they were "constantly hearing noise upstairs, even when there's no one up there," particularly footsteps.

In October 2011, BAUMALIRZ wrote a post on *Your Ghost Stories*, seeking support from other Fort Benning residents, reassurance that "I'm not just losing my mind." A month earlier she had joined her husband in Bouton Heights Village. Her first experience started when her husband left for PT in the early morning, when "the front door sounds like it opens and then shuts." Thinking her husband had returned for something, she looked out the window to find his car missing.

The couple had no children, but once, when she was alone, "I could swear I heard kid's footsteps running up and down the stairs."

Three days earlier, at 10 p.m., she was driving from Martin Army to Bouton Heights, through a secluded area with no buildings. As she turned onto Davis Hill she wrote, "I saw a woman, or man, with long black hair standing in the ditch on the side of the road." Taking a second look, "no one was there."

"I'm pretty freaked out," she wrote, reaching out to others with similar experiences at Fort Benning.

Many current and former residents of Fort Benning have told their stories on the *Ghosts of America* website.

Ronnie visited her daughter at Fort Benning and brought along a granddaughter, who "was constantly throwing up," during the visit. Ronnie burned seagrass sage and prayed, noting, "It calmed the spirits." She thought residents should do that every two weeks, with an application of holy water. She "saw and heard things" in her daughter's home and was "still in shock over the activity."

Lynn replied to Ronnie, stating that as a child, 1974–1977, her family had lived on base housing on Wickersham. "Things would disappear and reappear in weird places . . . My mom heard footsteps coming upstairs, but no one (was) there."

Anonymous also responded. During her Fort Benning residence on Wickersham, 1975–1977. "We had stuff happen too," primarily from "a maid's closet in the basement, weird stuff," like footsteps coming upstairs, "and doors would open for no reason."

"Your story is the most talked about in Fort Benning," she wrote, "and I believe every word." She had "just saged my daughter's room again. And opened doors this time. So spirits can go outside. Well, the doors started slamming."

Her theory on Fort Benning's hauntings: "Just think [of] all the history with the different wars and people who lived there. So much sadness and death with soldiers dying now and in the 1940s, energy sometimes stays."

She, her daughter, and her husband had another year's residence at Fort Benning, so their "story isn't over. I feel bad for the next families that move in," is a frequent sentiment from base residents.

ThirdIDwife had paranormal events at two different locations at Benning. She and her husband originally lived in Bouton Heights, where at night she would smoke out back. There was an empty dwelling with a burned kitchen and broken windows behind her home.

"I always got the feeling I was being watched and a couple times I caught movement from the upstairs windows."

She was initially happy to move to Arrowhead in Custer Village, but from the first day, "I feel like I am being watched all the time, I get the feeling someone's behind me when no one is there."

After ThirdIDwife's husband left for work in the morning, "I would hear someone walking around in boots and cabinet doors opening and closing, electronics go off and on." Although they had no children, "I've heard a young child crying." She had chills and her dogs barked at nothing. One day, "I saw a shadowy figure walk down the hallway."

The worst experience occurred as she was sitting in the living room watching TV, and she felt someone standing behind her. Whenever that occurred, one dog woke up, looked directly behind her and started "growling with all his hairs standing up!" Sometimes, both dogs simultaneously picked their heads up to "watch the same spot together as if someone is walking by."

On several occasions she quickly held up her phone and attempted to photograph the entity. That never worked because the phone would "go to the home screen or my phone will freeze or shut off automatically."

Leityn, her husband, and their son moved onto Craig Drive in Custer Village in August 2010. Within a month, stuff started occurring—at first, the normal phenomenon. She would hear her husband shut and lock the door as he left for PT at dawn, but she would later awake abruptly and walk to the top of the staircase "to find our living room door standing wide open."

Sometimes she and her husband would be in bed and "hear footsteps on the stairs or downstairs." Occasionally, when he was absent, she would hear the dryer door slam shut (with such force that she would ask her innocent husband, "Why are you so mad and slamming the dryer?"), and thrice she heard the oven timer go off.

Infantry soldiers graduate from Fort Benning in ceremonies held in these stands before deploying around the world. National Infantry Museum and Soldier Center.

The couple moved to Custer, where she continued to hear footsteps in the hall when alone. A visiting sister heard scratching and tapping on her wall at 1 a.m., audible over her TV.

In Bouton , Anonymous heard footsteps all the time, and a neighbor's daughter "was dragged out of her bed and had marks on her ankles." A different neighbor awoke to find "a woman pressing down on her chest." Cabinet doors opened and closed.

Ebony and her family lived in Indianhead Village in December 2010. Occasionally, "some freaky things happen," she wrote to *Ghosts of America*, including her two-year-old daughter staring at the closet in the master bedroom and saying, "Him, mama, him." Later, she was heard "screaming bloody murder" and pounding on a bedroom door begging to be admitted.

Ebony found the child had "pressed her little body up against the wall with a look so scared on her face she wouldn't take her eyes off our bedroom."

Ebony's husband almost threw out a plush toy that "went off by itself." One day her daughter's large pink ball "started to roll across the floor! It stopped dead in its tracks and rolled back to the chair, bounced off the chair leg (like someone or two of something were playing ball). I never been so freaked out."

Two nights before she posted, she and her daughter were sleeping together in bed when, "I saw a yellowish fog" that apparently entered the little girl, who "woke up screaming, yelling 'something bit me mama!' I looked at her arm and it looked discolored." The discoloration quickly vanished.

On *Ghosts of America*'s (GOA) website, Anonymous described a visit to a friend at Fort Benning. After everyone else was asleep, she decided to watch TV in bed until she nodded off. She was shortly awakened to see "all the doors in the room open: bedroom door, bathroom door, closet door (with the light on), and also the drawers of both night stands open."

Finding everyone else asleep, "I was really freaking out," she wrote, "convinced there is something not right about the house."

Girlygirl was watching a movie on TV with her family when "suddenly all the lights went out." The family collectively trooped to the garage to find the power box open.

Worse yet, she encountered a little girl who "told me her name, which was Susan, and she always talks to me." The family still lives there, "because Susan doesn't bother us."

Another afflicted family consisted of Lindsey, her husband, and their two children. It all started one night as Lindsey put her newborn down, tucked two-year-old Hayden in, and retired to her own bed. Hearing a loud crash in Hayden's room, she rushed to him, fearing that he had climbed on his dresser and it had fallen on him. She found the dresser upright and Hayden "sitting straight up in his bed pointing to the dresser against my wall. He would not say anything."

One morning, Lindsey's bathroom routine was interrupted when Hayden ran in saying, "there's a scary man sitting on the couch." Suspecting an intruder, she rushed to the living room, Hayden too frightened to follow. No one was on the couch, and when Hayden saw this, he looked confused.

Several times Lindsey "would wake up around midnight hearing my two-year-old talking to someone." Thinking he was safely in bed, she found "him sitting in the dark sitting on the cold tile in the living room having a conversation with someone." Normally, Hayden was frightened by the dark.

In early February, Lindsey asked Hayden who his Valentine was at daycare. "Katie," he said—who had red air. When Lindsey asked at the school, teachers said there was no Katie and no girl with red hair.

"My son would randomly tell me he was playing with Katie in his room, and she was nice," Hayden would say casually, but what came next horrified her. The boy "told me Katie has black hair, but it's red from all the blood and that she told him the man hurts her." Lindsey was shocked. There should be no way a two-year-old should be able to describe something so terrible.

Another shocking detail emerged when Hayden announced that under his bed was a man with red eyes. When she showed him there was no one there, "he always argued and said there was a man there." During the same week, Lindsey's two dogs, who usually slept with her, "stood in the hallway and growled with their heads down looking under my bed." For a week the canines refused to enter the room.

When her family was visiting from Florida, Hayden played happily on the floor with a toy truck. Suddenly, they realized, "he was frozen, staring at the corner of the living room." Hayden ran to his mother and buried his face in her shoulder, saying,

"There is a scary man near the door." She assured him no one was there, but when he looked, "his eyes began to follow something moving from the corner of the room towards him. As it walked to us, my son looked up at it and screamed "No!" He began crying, "No mommy, I don't want to touch him."

Lindsey's husband grabbed a camera and started snapping shots of the scene. One picture showed "two glowing eyes . . . in the exact spot my son said" the man was.

That was the last straw. The family moved from their house of terror.

Apryl moved with her family to a three-bedroom residence, dating to the 1930s, in Custer Village. The first night there, she "was scared of this house," although she had never felt that way at any other home. She "started hearing unexplained creaks and sounds," particularly from her closet, but only when the rest of her family was asleep. The noise kept her "up at all hours of the night."

"I heard footsteps as most people who lived over Custer do," she continued. Her daughter was afraid of her bedroom, claiming there was a mean girl there.

Apryl's husband considered her crazy because he never experienced any phenomenon. The other wives said they "had the same thing happening to them, but none of their husbands heard anything at all."

One wife several doors down left her phone recording in her hall while she sat quietly in the living room. As "they played it back they heard several voices and loud crashing and booming sounds," although nothing was heard while the sounds were being recorded.

After an argument one night, her husband drove to King Pond to cool off as he watched the water. At one point, he spotted a shadowy figure sitting on the bank. Periodically, he saw "what appeared to be a cherry of a cigarette that would glow as if someone were taking a drag." The figure disappeared two minutes later.

"I believe that this base is very haunted," Apryl wrote. "I can feel the negative and eerie energy all around. Everyone seems to hate this base, and not one of us can explain why." She thought the base depressing, "and I blame it on the ghosts or the incident that happened here in the 1970s," presumably a reference to a controversial UFO incident described in depth later.

L lived on Stone Court in Bouton Heights. A cabinet popped open, the microwave oven beeped "like someone setting cook time," an interior door "likes to open itself," and "occasionally I'll hear the front door open and close." Also, the dog "starts freaking out and barking at the back windows." As she sat up late watching TV, "I'll hear someone coming downstairs," when her husband was sleeping soundly. "I very rarely feel like I'm alone even if I'm the only one in the house."

Anonymous lived in a barracks apartment on Kelley Hill with a roommate. Alone one Christmas season, he was awakened by hearing "the outside door slam." He heard nothing else and the door was securely locked.

An organized person by nature, he awoke one morning to "find my closet door open with all of my ACUs laying in the middle of my floor."

He and his buddies liked to sit around the pond, spotting alligators. One night they heard "hound dogs barking." After five minutes, they spotted a lantern light in the woods. All at once the dogs were silenced and the light extinguished. The phenomenon occurred several other times. Perhaps an old-time resident was hunting with his similarly old dogs.

In 1996, Amendez lived on Terry Drive while her husband served in Korea. Because she was anxious about the cemetery across the street, she kept her living room blinds closed. One day while watching TV, she checked the time on a pendulum clock positioned in front of that window. Thirty minutes later, she looked at it again, only to find "the clock was turned around." This occurred several times, and her mother "told me to move the clock because the spirits didn't like it sitting there." She did and the clock no longer shifted position.

Concerned for the family's safety with her husband absent, "I installed alarms on the doors and windows that with a turn of a key was armed." One night she locked the deadbolt, kept the key with her, and put the children to bed. Hours later she was awakened by her blaring stereo in the living room. Investigating, she found her four-year-old daughter, sound asleep, standing at the front door, which was wide open. Amendez locked up, reset the alarm, put the girl back to bed, and checked the house for intruders, but found none.

This unsettling event occurred three more times, and she "couldn't understand how (the child) got the door open with everything set." Amendez concluded that "some bad entity was trying to get my daughter to go out the door, but the good spirits turned the stereo on each time to wake me up to find her standing in the door."

One night as she lay awake, "I felt a bad presence in my bedroom . . . I was paralyzed and had a terrifying feeling come over me." Suddenly, a music box, that was never wound and had to be manually activated, began to play.

"When the music stopped it sounded as if something was trying to crash through my ceiling."

Amendez had Nagel prints hanging on a living room wall, but was disturbed when "the children used to have conversations with these pictures." When she asked who they were speaking with, "they would tell me the ladies in the pictures. It was strange to hear a one-sided conversation as if listening to the kids on a telephone conversation."

At this time, cracks appeared in that wall and her "daughter started having unexplained seizures." Amendez heard strange sounds, lights turned on and off, and cabinet doors and drawers opened and closed. Fortunately, "everything stopped when my husband returned from Korea." She feared they "were the only ones who experienced these things" until she discovered the *Ghosts of America* website.

This statue honors Lt. Rich Rescorla, whose actions at Ia Drag in Vietnam in 1965 epitomizes the soldiers' code, "Leave No Man behind." National Infantry Museum and Soldier Center.

La and her husband had no children when they moved to Fort Benning, so it seemed strange to wake up one night after a three-year residence to hear "what sounded like a child talking to someone." The couple was startled and their cat "was in a state of high alert." It was 4:48 on a Monday morning. Thinking a neighbor's baby monitor was on the same band as their cordless phone, La checked with her neighbors; no one had such a monitor.

Two weeks later, again at 4:48 on a Monday morning, "we heard furniture being moved across the hardwood floors." After La's husband deployed several months later, she heard the printer, unused since they arrived. Investigating, she found the "printer button was off and it was printing like someone has pushed the print command. Weird."

Lights have "turned on and off by themselves," and there were "an occasional set of footsteps."

Tori's story started like so many others. She and her husband lived on Craig Court in Custer Village. One morning, fifteen minutes after he left for PT, "I heard the front door open and shut." Tori texted him, asking what he had forgotten. He replied that he "was in the parking lot waiting for PT to start.

"I was so scared I stayed in the bed until he got back!" Tori said. During the day, when the front door was open, "I see what seems to be shadows walking by outside, but nobody is there." She also heard the door to the laundry room open and close.

A neighbor and her husband "have heard wet footsteps in their bedroom," and they hear their daughter scream from her bed only to find the child "sound asleep."

Dawn had a unique experience. On Custer Terrace in 2000, she awoke from deep sleep to find a man standing at the foot of her bed. She described "a black man with blue overalls," and no shirt. "I just froze," she recounted, but then dismissed it as a trick of her mind. However, by the time they moved in 2001, "I had seen him in the same place five more times." She thought the man had been a slave. There had been slaves on the property of Fort Benning, but the figure could also have been a more recent sharecropper or a farm owner.

Cici said, "there is always a soldier walking around our house. Me, my mom, and my brothers have seen him or felt him around a lot. He doesn't really hurt anybody. He just walks around looking for something and disappears." Footsteps were heard in the attic, and tapping came from windows.

Ccj's husband lived on Gibson in Custer Village, while she initially remained in California. Her husband "would feel like someone was watching him, hear footsteps, our doors would slam, and our front door and screen would open at times."

Although she found these reports alarming, she soon joined him. Her first experience was hearing "what would sound like sticky bare feet walking in our house. I would feel someone lying next to me in bed; something would move my pillow when I tried to sleep."

Her military police (MP) husband would make a quick trip home to grab a meal while on duty, and sometimes, "I would hear what sounded like the front door opening and boots walking in and out of my house." She called him to say she would gladly bring his food outside, but on each occasion he told her he had not been home.

"I do not think 'it' likes my husband so much," Ccj believed. "He has gotten pushed and choked." Knowing "I had 'guests' in the house," she attempted to coexist by asking it "to stay in the guest room." Bad idea.

As all couples do, the young people argued occasionally, and once, "things got bad. He went and slept in our spare bedroom and I heard him choking. The door was locked and I started screaming for him to open the door. He opened it while gasping for air. I slid him out of the room and helped him onto the couch."

Her husband was mumbling, and when Ccj asked what was wrong, "he yelled in a strange voice, 'That's my room.'" He shouted this three times. She thought she should "sit on top of him and pray," and that tactic worked. Recovering, he remembered nothing, asking "how he'd gotten into the living room."

Her sister-in-law came for a visit, sleeping in the guest room, but that was not where her supernatural event occurred. She placed her phone on the bathroom counter and got into the tub. The resident spirit "threw the phone off the counter and tried to hit my sister-in-law. She ran out of the bathroom in a towel screaming."

"I am convinced my house is haunted," Ccj concluded.

She also admitted that while growing up, she "had played with Ouija boards" and "experienced some very strange things."

A family living on Squires Lane in Custer Village heard slamming doors, dryer doors that popped open and shut, and each day at 11:59 p.m., "we would hear a little girl laugh."

Dkh's family lived first on McGraw Manor, then Arrowhead Road, where they had "some seriously strange experiences." One night at 2 a.m., she heard the sound of, "war drums, Native American drums," as if from a distance. She awakened her husband for reassurance, but he dismissed it as bass from a passing car stereo cranked up loud.

Two weeks later both were awake when the sound returned. This time he admitted that "it sounded like war drums," far away, but each beat still clearly audible.

After putting her son on the school bus in the morning, a neighbor approached and asked if she had heard a drum at 1 a.m.

The drumming stopped afterward. Perhaps construction on Fort Benning land had unearthed ancient graves. Certainly Native Americans had occupied the land along the Chattahoochee River for millennia, and construction of the base surely disturbed many burials.

Dkh wrote a second post describing one night, with her son abed and she rocking her daughter in the living room while hubby worked as an MP. The little girl had just fallen asleep, "when I heard little footsteps running down the hall."

She thought it was her son, but he never appeared and she found him sleeping soundly. Those were her first phantom footsteps, and "although I didn't see the 'child' that night, I did see him later during another encounter," looking three or four years old and dressed in late eighteenth-century clothing. The ghost hid occasionally and turned "on my son's battery powered toys from time to time."

Reanne moved to McKibben Court and experienced ghostly activity her first week.

"I've seen a lady in a white dress in my room," she wrote. Unafraid, she said casually, "'What's up lady in white?' and went back to sleep."

Another night, a little boy not only appeared but straddled her. "Again I said, 'What's up little boy?' but he stayed on me for a while," and she grew apprehensive, then panicked and screamed, afterward wondering how anyone could sleep in that house.

Her four-year-old nephew, who awoke crying each morning between two and three, "said there is a man in the bath of this house who shot himself in the head."

For ten years, Christine had driven a taxi that often transported soldiers from Fort Benning. One year into that job she had picked up a soldier who was not sure of his destination, but wanted to enter Columbus.

"He was on crutches and his leg was bandaged," she said. He told me that he had misjudged a landing earlier in the day and rolled his ankle."

During the trip the uniformed man fell silent, which Christine attributed to fatigue. After a bit she needed to know his destination. "I turned to speak and he wasn't there. We hadn't stopped, not even at a traffic light. It's always baffled me to this day."

Transporting ghosts unaware is a common phenomenon in supernatural circles.

In August 1991, Rick was an MP K-9 officer patrolling the southern part of Fort Benning with Tippo, his security dog. They had inspected the Fryar Field drop zone and he was driving to the Uchee Creek Campground when he spotted a man walking in the ditch in front of him. He slowed and the guy looked like a soldier wearing an unfamiliar uniform. As Rick passed, he scrutinized the walker, who ignored the MP, "as if he was intent on being somewhere."

"Gray trousers," he described the individual's uniform, "a brownish-tan button-down jacket, a belt, boots, hat with a small bill, carrying a musket style rifle, and a knapsack draped over his shoulder."

After passing the soldier, Rick decided he should take a second look. Quickly turning around, he saw no one, "just a lot of ground steam and a very cool feeling in the air."

When Rick stopped, Tippo, "who's not afraid of anything," whined and refused to leave the truck. Man and dog "got the *&%$ out of there fast, stayed on main post the rest of the night."

Sidney lived in McGraw Village at Benning with her parents and a brother. She often heard "running up and down the stairs," and once she and a friend saw odd entities. The friend "saw something short and white walk into the bathroom," while she "saw a black figure of a man standing behind me." After going to bed they heard footsteps and a door open and close. In the morning, her mother said her bedroom door had been mysteriously opened and closed.

As she washed dishes, Sidney again saw the black male figure standing behind her. When she turned toward it, the image vanished. On a third occasion, while in her room listening to music, "a black figure stood right in front of me."

As a child, in 1988, Alex was getting into bed when an "older man appeared in blue jeans and a brownish jacket." The boy closed his eyes and wished the man away. The intruder was gone when Alex opened his eyes, and he raced to find his parents.

Robert lived on Miller Loop with his parents and two sisters. He believed that their house was haunted by two different entities, "a man, probably thirty-five to forty years old, wearing clothes from sixty to eighty years ago, and a little girl. The man stands at the top of the stairs when you see him. He also walked down the hall.

"The little girl loves to play with things. My little sister says her stuffed animals get moved around along with some of her other toys."

A variety of vehicles that America's infantry have used over the years are displayed at the National Infantry Museum and Soldier Center.

The girl ran down the hall to bother his mother, and his older sister had her own encounter when the girl was standing behind Robert. As "my sister looked at the little girl, she said she smiled back, as if she was saying, 'You caught me!'"

Robert lived in the basement, which the ghosts generally avoided. He heard "knocking on my windows, and a soldier running up our house stairs and ringing the bell, then stomping off 'cause no one answered.'" Only he and the older sister heard the bell or steps. The family lived easily with the spirits, because "they don't attack us, harm us, or scare us."

In 2005, Cami lived with her husband and two children in Bouton Heights, where they witnessed "many instances of unexplainable encounters." She once returned home to find "there was trash spread all in the hallway almost as if an animal or something got in it." There had been no animals or people in the house.

After Cami's husband deployed in 2006, she felt there was another person in the house and "started seeing a man in the hallway." The ghost was in her dreams, "and he wanted to hurt me," she thought. She nailed carpet to the stairs because, "I would just all of a sudden lose my footing and fall down," a problem which only occurred during this period.

One night the house so frightened her that she took refuge in a neighbor's home. Returning for diapers, she found the door, securely locked when she departed, open, with a candlestick thrown to the floor.

Cami once found herself "locked" in her pantry, and in the night heard "harsh footsteps in the hallway upstairs. I know that something went on here; the man that is here does not like females, because I only have trouble when my husband has duty or is in the field or deployed."

Cami called her situation "scary and weird" and could not wait to leave. However, she felt "sorry for the next family that lives here."

Lokyden "experienced several ghost sightings in my house," at Bouton Heights. Once, when he walked to the front door and started to open it, "all of a sudden a hand came out and slammed the door shut. I ran outside." When he made PX [post exchange] runs at night, he sometimes returned to see "a man standing in my window."

One night, while living in Custer Terrace, Michelle was irritated when her "little boy jumped into bed with me." She started into the, "You're too old for this" speech and returned him to his own room, which she found "ice cold," and "felt the most evil presence" surrounding them, a sensation she had never experienced before.

They ran back to her room and leaped into bed, the boy "shaking and too scared to cry . . . so I just prayed out loud!" until the boy screamed, "Shut up, Mommy, you're making it worse. Shut up!" The youngster had never addressed her that way.

"I was terrified!" she wrote. "I could literally feel the separation between my spirit and my body! I started cussing at it, and it went away," although she could "hear it in the rafters," as if the timbers were moving.

Michelle wanted to attribute the experience to over-active imaginations, but a neighbor "said she had a similar experience." She went to the chaplain for guidance, and a priest "came to our place and placed holy water over every entrance and window."

They had no further trouble there, but when they moved to another house on Arrowhead Road, there were "constant bad dreams" when her husband was absent.

During a barbecue, "my daughter came running in saying, 'Mommy, there is a mean man bothering me.'" No one was there, but then the "dog's ears stood up, and we heard the back screen doorknob turn, the door opened and slammed shut!" Her husband raced outside but saw nothing, and no one was present.

"We were really freaked!" noted Michelle. When she asked the child to describe the intruder, the girl said, "he had boots and a funny hat," perhaps a soldier's beret?

Spc was a soldier who lived on Guenette Court in Bouton Heights for two years with his wife and two daughters. He described "weird things" that happened, including the dryer door opening by night and day, and footsteps upstairs while the family was all gathered downstairs. He and his wife "fought about things we wouldn't fight about" and separated for three months.

While Spc was at work, their six-year-old thought she saw him walking downstairs, describing the figure as "a shadow shaped like a man."

Their dogs refused to take a straight path down a hallway and insisted on going through other rooms to access the kitchen. Sometimes they would go "on guard" and "herd the family into the living room and one would circle us while the other stood guard in the hallway."

J., a resident of Davis Hill, spoke to a new neighbor who had just moved from Bouton Heights and learned, "they had really bad things go on there." As the couple and their son slept, they heard "a loud, harsh growl from the foot of the bed." At different times, "a man came out of her closet, and then on other nights opened the closet and went back in."

J. said at times she thought she heard her husband downstairs when he was not home.

On Rainbow Avenue, Fe was watching TV downstairs when, "I heard a bloodcurdling scream just outside the house." She rushed upstairs to check on her mother, who thought Fe had screamed. They checked on neighbors finding them all well.

Another day, again watching TV, "I noticed movement out of the corner of my eye." She looked in that direction and "saw something that froze me to the spot. My mother collects porcelain dolls (which is creepy enough on its own) and had two mounted on wall stands by the front door. When I looked . . . one of the dolls seemingly was pulled from the stand, came out to the middle of the entrance, flipped over, and [was] placed face up on the floor," without a sound. "I was terrified!" she said.

Fe summarized, "Beautiful houses, creepy place."

The history of all Americans who have served in the infantry is explored at the National Infantry Museum and Soldier Center.

A appealed on GOA for people who might have previously lived in their home on Arrowhead Road in Custer Village to contact her, because "I believe there is something going on here. I have terrible nightmares I cannot wake up from," every night that her husband was absent, she wrote. Sometimes she "could not stop crying," and once had "the feeling of being choked."

More recently, "when he is gone, I wake up to hear something walking and dragging something down the hallway away from the bedroom to the front door."

A feared she lived in one of the houses previously written about as haunted. In conclusion, "I am sure this being Fort Benning that many things could have happened in these old houses or to the people that lived in them."

Tia hadn't seen a ghost, just experienced "strange things." She and her husband returned to find a picture "ripped from a wall" with considerable force. Cabinet doors and drawers closed themselves, and a new dog sat and stared at nothing. A visiting friend left her glasses on a table and returned to find a lens missing.

In April 2010, Jackay and her family were excited to be assigned to a newly remodeled home on Arrowhead Road. They had spent the previous five years in an old rundown house on Valdez that was demolished. The problems started their first night, Jackay wrote Ghosts of America.

As she watched TV, she heard her youngest son call for her, only to find him deeply asleep. Jackay discovered lights, which had been turned off, brightly burning, but she was most disturbed to find her Great Dane staring at a hall, his hair standing up. The growling dog stood protectively in front of her.

She decided the odds were against both her and the dog "being crazy at the same time." The dog also would not enter her bedroom, even for a treat.

In late May, as her oldest son played DS in bed, "something pushed his video game at his face."

Jackay complained to the housing authority that "something wasn't right" at her house, but they discounted her story.

In early July, her husband woke in the night and went out for a three-minute smoke. Every light in the house (save nightlights) had been off when he started his break, but when he returned every light was on. Later that week he was awakened by a handle on their dresser knocking itself against the wood. He subsequently apologized for calling his wife crazy.

These problems were insignificant, however, compared to what happened next. From the day they moved in, "I started feeling very sick," Jackay said. She would compile a thick file of documented medical proof. On August 15, 2011, Jackay was "pale, barely able to stand and my heart was about to pound out of my chest." At the base hospital, she was admitted with a blood court of five, requiring an emergency transfusion of blood.

She felt better in the hospital, but not at home, where within hours she was again sick and vomiting. Three weeks later she was back in the hospital for another blood transfusion. Her primary doctor thought she was bleeding internally. A number of doctors "tested me for hundreds of diseases," but found nothing.

Jackay visited Kansas City for two weeks, felt better, and found her blood count at 9.5. Back home at Benning, she fell ill yet again, "while doors are still opening, lights are turned on, my kids are scared to death of the thing in their room, and my dog is freaking out" daily. She found knickknacks from a wall shelf shattered to pieces on the floor, and a number of angel statues were broken.

Jackay's blood count was 7.3 on October 22, and she was asked to return several days later, when the count was six and she required another blood transfusion and a three-day hospital stay. Still, every test failed to find a cause.

She felt well enough to leave the hospital, but started taking precautions at home, spending as much time as possible outdoors. That worked, but back in the house she grew sick and returned to the hospital for yet another transfusion. She spent most of November and December outside, but as winter approached she was forced to remain inside for longer periods. On December 19, she was at the doctor's office with a blood count of 7.3.

Jackay returned home angry. Inside, she found her couch moved and lights on. "I snapped and told whatever or whoever was in my house to f^&* itself, stop waking up my husband, stop tearing up my stuff, scaring my kids, and freaking out my dog, and that they could kiss my ass. I was pissed because I wasn't feeling well."

Within two hours she was desperately sick. While shopping the next day, she felt much better, but grew ill again at home. Two days later, her husband took her to the hospital, because "it felt like something invisible was stabbing me." She was too sick to walk.

Doctors at the hospital found her blood critically low, 4.5, and concluded she must be bleeding internally, so much that she would have died without an immediate transfusion. She couldn't "move, see, hear, feel, there was nothing but darkness," and she did almost die.

"Doctors did CTs, MRIs, a colonoscopy, shoved a tube down my throat, ultrasounds on every part of me." No problems were detected, stunning the doctors and her family. Jackay recorded that the medical professionals found nothing and freely admitted they could find no reason for her suffering.

Throughout this ordeal, Jackay realized, all her indoor flowers died, despite her best efforts.

When the family moved from Fort Benning to Kansas on January 18, her doctor gave her a complete record of the case for her new physician. Jackay had her blood tested the following day; it was 9. On February 24, it was 12.

As she left Benning, Jackay begged housing personnel to not place another family in their house, "but they probably will."

Potential paratroopers usually dreaded their first experience of the jump towers at Eubanks Field. Four were constructed in the early 1940s, and several remain today as prominent Fort Benning landmarks. Recruits, strapped to a harness and parachute, were raised 200 feet into the air and released to float back to the ground.

In the mid-1960s, according to Faith Serafin in *Haunted Columbus, Georgia, Phantoms of the Fountain City*, the rigging on one student snapped, allowing the soldier to plummet to earth from a height of sixty feet, resulting in two broken arms, one broken leg, and injuries to his ribs and face. He succumbed to complications from his injuries several weeks later.

Soon lights were mysteriously activated in the elevator houses, and essential equipment disappeared just before it was needed. Accidents at the towers increased, leading to their closure.

Tales of the phantom of Eubanks Field continued to grow, with reports of paranormal activity in surrounding neighborhoods and the airborne barracks. There were "sightings of an unusual soldier in an out-of-date uniform walking with a strange kink in his step," Serafin wrote.

During a fire drill at 4 a.m., a sergeant patrolled the barracks to ensure that all soldiers had safely exited. He was alarmed to find a man lying face down in one building. The soldier lay in an awkward position, and "his face had been crushed. Blood and bone fragments were scattered all over the floor." The sergeant ran to summon help, but when he returned the injured man had disappeared, and so had every trace of blood and bone.

A four-year-old boy saw a similar figure peering at him through his window. The alarmed mother summoned MPs, who searched the area fruitlessly. The topper was that the boy's room was located on the second story, twenty feet above the ground.

Ghosts of Eubanks Field stories have circulated for half a century. Lights continue to flash near the jump towers, and a ghostly figure walks the area and vanishes before startled witnesses. Perhaps the paratrooper wishes to complete his training before reporting to his final post.

The Station Hospital opened in 1925. During World War II, the facility treated 3,600 men for battlefield wounds, injuries, and illnesses. Each received care from numerous female nurses. When Martin Army Hospital opened in 1958, Station Hospital continued service as a clinic. In 1977, the building opened as the National Infantry Museum, filled with a large collection of historic army artifacts and displays. These were transferred to the new museum in 2009, and the former Station Hospital has been converted for yet another purpose.

According to Serafin, the best known ghost story related to the building concerns two Murphy brothers, both critically wounded fighting in Germany. The first to arrive, suffering from gangrene, was excited to hear that his brother would be arriving soon, but he died before the anticipated reunion. The second brother had also looked forward to seeing his sibling. Learning on arrival that his brother had died, he passed within days.

These brothers have been witnessed, both wearing their World War II uniforms, playing cards together—the sound of shuffling cards audible—and walking together through the halls, happily conversing.

Another reported ghost mystery is a soldier wearing a Confederate uniform, although no Civil War activity occurred on Fort Benning property. He was observed examining artifacts kept in storage and disappeared with the transfer of historic material to the new museum. Perhaps he was spiritually attached to one of the Civil War artifacts once held here.

A female spirit, a reddish-blonde clad in a hospital gown, was "in a rather sickly state, her pale skin riddled with sores that appeared to be open and bleeding," Serafin wrote. She might have suffered from measles in an age when that was a deadly affliction. This ghost roams the halls and enters rooms and balconies, appearing and disappearing.

A final female spirit that is only audible is thought to be a World War II nurse. The story is that she had a crush on a doctor, who spurned her affection. Distraught, she threw herself off an upper story of the nurse's barracks. Her screams reverberate through the building.

Four men working on the latest reconstruction of the structure heard moans in the east wing as they prepared to exit one evening. When the sounds recurred for several days, they searched the building, finding nothing.

Gijoe_99 and his battle buddy "were pulling barracks guard duty during basic training," he wrote the ghost story website: *Castle of Spirits.*

His battalion was nicknamed Devil's Playground, but, according to legend, it had been changed from House of Pain several years earlier because, according to legend, "they had three Pvts [privates] commit suicide during one training cycle during one program called 'High Stress Training.'

"At night some guys said they'd hear noises coming from the platoon bay below us. Usually, it sounded like the platoon was receiving remedial training," or punishment for deficient performance.

The night of his supernatural experience, Gijoe_99 was pulling guard duty "in the furthest (and darkest) end of the bay." It was 1:15 a.m. when "the platoon below us started doing mule kicks in the bay," which "was impossible since the rest of the company was off" on leave, "and our bay was the only one occupied in the entire battalion!"

The exercise continued for ten minutes. He spent the remainder of his duty with his partner at the doors, where most guards usually congregated, "for different reasons," but most probably because it was "in the light."

Gijoe_99 didn't know the history of the barracks, but "being part of the Infantry Training Brigade, I can imagine that quite a lot of negative energy has been left in those hallowed halls." A popular motto there was, "Pain is weakness leaving the body (and we're gonna' lose a whole lotta' weakness)."

Peter Brooks joined the US Army in 2008 and was sent to Fort Benning. Soldiers spend the first few weeks in 30AG (30th Adjutant General Reception Battalion) getting processed before reporting to basic training.

The Vietnam Memorial Plaza at the National Infantry Museum and Soldier Center.

One night at 3 a.m., Brooks was on watch, patrolling the barracks to ensure that everyone was asleep in their bunks, a one-hour duty that all recruits pulled.

Bored, he decided to clean the bathroom. He had just cleaned out his bucket in the shower and went to a sink to wash the grime off his hands. Glancing up into the mirror, he saw a bright orb shoot past him. Then, in the ear on the side of the orb, he heard a young man, possibly a teenager, say, "Hello," in a cherry voice.

Badly frightened, he hurried to wake his replacement and got into bed.

Reflecting on the experience, Brooks thought of two possible scenarios for the ghostly voice. He learned that there were always recruits who quickly learned that they had made a bad mistake by enlisting. Some of these unfortunate young men took their own lives.

Also, men killed in combat might remember their last good memories as 30AG, and so their spirits might return.

On September 3, 2014, Brooks published his account on YouTube with a video titled *My SCARY Fort Benning Ghost Experience*. He had never believed in the supernatural or the existence of ghosts before, but this encounter "changed his mindset," he said.

One of the most recent Fort Benning ghost stories was submitted to *Ghosts of America* by TDY in November 2015. By the way, TDY means "Temporary Duty Assignment," although in the South we call it "Temporary Duty Yonder."

After a long day of briefings and classes at Fort Benning, TDY elected to forego dinner with colleagues and returned to his hotel room, located near the National Infantry Museum, to study for a college exam.

At one point he "heard a horse in the hallway." Thinking it must be a movie playing in another room, he returned to his studies. Next, he heard what sounded like a horse stomping the ground. The noise was repeated again from a point down the hall. TDY attempted to open his door to investigate, but "it seemed as if something kicked my door."

He called the night manager, but she could scarcely hear him because, "I was literally screaming in the phone."

He asked for someone to investigate what he called a stuck door. As he waited, another thunderous kick struck a different part of the door.

After the woman arrived, the door was truly stuck, refusing to open. When his TV abruptly came on, "I was ready to break the window," to exit the room, TDY wrote.

After the manager left to summon maintenance, "the door made an unlocking click noise," and easily opened.

TDY went to the front office and saw a giant black spider hanging from the ceiling. He used a flip flop to knock it to the floor before crushing the arachnid and a number of tiny baby spiders that erupted from their mother's body.

"Then, the woman and I heard a loud trotting down the road," audible even inside the hotel.

TDY resolved to never return to that hotel, and possibly Fort Benning.

Another recent report was written by Lysh. She, her active-duty husband, and their two-year-old son lived in Bouton Heights on Devore Court.

During their first few months' residence, she heard footsteps on the bare wooden stairs, usually between 1:30 and 3:30 in the morning. Her real fear started while her husband spent a week in the field. Curiously, she noted that the steps were never heard at the top or bottom of the stairs, but only on the middle of the staircase.

One night, "to prove to myself that there isn't anything there I poured baby powder in the middle of the stairs when I went up for bed."

As she fell asleep she heard the steps on the stairs. When they ceased, "I got up to check . . . I walked over to the stairs, and there it was. A couple of footprints in the baby powder; I was scared then, but I learned to live with it."

The footsteps ceased while her mother-in-law and her children visited and never returned. Unfortunately, something far more sinister developed.

After she and her husband woke up in the middle of the night, they heard their son in his bedroom, yelling as if he were angry. Opening his door, she found him "sitting up in his bed yelling, 'NO! STOP!'" but nothing was visible. She hugged the boy and when she turned on the light he again yelled "NO!"

In bed with his parents, the child "yelled at whatever was there. I said to leave my family alone and whoever was there isn't wanted and should leave. Since then I haven't heard anything." However, they "do still see black shadows at the corner of our eyes. "

Time Slips

One night in 2008, Chris and her husband drove around the base, killing time and enjoying the cool air. They were on a wooded back road near the landing strip when, "an old 1940s-era army truck drove by us . . . It was olive green with wooden side rails with approximately twenty or thirty men sitting in the back. The men were wearing green uniforms like the ones they wore in World War II, with hard helmets on their heads."

After it passed, the couple glanced at each other and said, "Wait a minute . . . something felt weird about that."

They immediately turned around and started speeding to locate the truck, but found nothing. The couple described this truly strange encounter as "peculiar." They "never saw a vehicle like it anywhere on Fort Benning."

In Trent's work at Fort Benning, he traversed the entire base, often exiting near the airport, where there is a "blinking sign that warns you of a plane landing." One day, with the lights not flashing, "out of nowhere a plane that resembled an old C-130 in faded primer grey flew over my truck as if it was headed for a landing on the strip."

Seconds later, he stopped to watch the plane land, but "there was no plane in sight." It had not landed, nor was it in a hangar or still flying. Stranger still, he had experienced the same event earlier that day.

"I'm sorry," Trent wrote, "but c130's don't just disappear . . . Or do they?!" Maybe they do, and it seems they reappear as well, much like the phantom troop truck.

After reading Trent's account, Tori explained that she and a friend had been at "Fryar Field watching the airborne students jump." On their way back, "we heard a plane right behind, which we thought was going over us, and when we looked," there was no plane. "So weird and freaky," she commented.

UFOs

The US Government sponsored programs to study UFOs. Its primary effort started in 1952 and was named Project Blue Book. The program continued for nearly twenty years. In 1969, it concluded that UFOs posed no threat to American security. Of 12,000 sightings investigated, most were declared identified, even if some excuses were not quite credible. The air force admitted that 585 cases were unidentified, including several that involved Fort Benning.

BLUE BOOK CASE # 868

At 10 p.m., on January 12, 1951, Second Lieutenant A. C. Hale, stationed at Fort Benning, saw a light with a fan-shaped wake that hovered motionless for twenty minutes before it instantly accelerated and flew out of sight.

PILOT CHASES A UFO

The files of Project Blue Book are preserved in the National Archives. One case details a substantial encounter by an air force pilot with a UFO.

Lieutenant George H. Kinmon, Jr., a World War II veteran, lifted off from Lawson Army Airfield at Fort Benning at 11:40 p.m. on July 9, 1951. At 3:30, near Dearing, twenty-five miles west of Augusta, his F-51 Mustang fighter-bomber was level at 8,500 feet on a course of 247 degrees and making 270 miles an hour.

Kinmon soon encountered a white object that dived out of the sun. It was "completely round and spinning in a clockwise direction," and made multiple passes at his plane.

According to quotes from an air force intelligence document:

Object described as flat on top and bottom and appearing from a front view to have rounded edges and slightly beveled . . . No vapor trails or exhaust or visible system of propulsion. Described as traveling at tremendous speed . . . object dived from the sun in front and under the plane and continued to barrel-roll around the plane for a period of ten minutes, when it disappeared under the plane . . . object was 300 to 400 feet from plane and appeared to be 10 to 15 feet in diameter. Pilot states he felt disturbance in the air described as "bump" when object passed under plane . . . Pilot considered by associates to be highly reliable, of mature judgment, and a creditable observer. Pilot notified tower, Robins AFB by radio and contacted flight service at Maxwell Air Force Base (Montgomery, Alabama) . . . Pilot unable to take photo due to camera malfunction.

As the object dove, Kinmon "noted small spots on the object that he described as being similar to craters on the moon through high-powered telescope." It did not seem to be aluminum and traveled at "tremendous speed."

The object disengaged at a point between Milledgeville and Macon.

The pilot, who had flown since 1942, had accumulated 1,500 hours flying time and flew combat missions over Europe in 1944–1945.

This UFO exhibited highly aggressive behavior. Diving from the sun is the best way to ambush another aircraft, the barrel rolling showed it as a superior craft with a daring pilot, and the camera malfunction is typical of many paranormal encounters.

BLUE BOOK CASE # 2365

A second substantial UFO\pilot encounter occurred on January 28, 1953. Major Hal W. Lamb, the senior pilot at Moody Air Force Base in Valdosta, took off in an F-86 Sabre jet fighter for a routine flight northwest to Fort Benning's Lawson Field, where he was to turn east to Robins Air Force Base and return home to Moody. Soon after landing, the pilot's encounter was taped by Edward Ruppert, head of Blue Book.

At 9:15 p.m., the pilot was over Albany. Looking up into the sky, he spotted an unusually bright white light at the ten o'clock position. After watching it for several minutes, he thought it must be either a distant airplane, the red and green lights on its wing tips invisible, or a star. The problem with those ideas was the object's circular shape.

Because Lamb was not on a specific mission, but simply accumulating flight hours, he decided to close on the UFO. After checking his oxygen, he started a climb from 6,000 feet to 30,000 feet. He was above the object four minutes later to find it had changed position in relation to the stars, proving it was not a star or other celestial body, making it a probable airplane, he thought.

The pilot then descended to close with the craft. He was successful as the light grew larger. Suddenly the white light changed colors, to red and then back to white. This cycle occurred every two seconds. He also noted that it shifted shape from circular to a perfect triangle, then the object divided into two triangles, one above the other. Transformation completed, the object vanished instantly.

"It was just like someone turning off a light," Lamb stated, "it's there, and then it's gone."

As the pilot neared Lawson Field at Fort Benning, he checked his gauges and found that his actions had consumed much of his fuel, leaving him unable to fly to both Robins and Moody. He decided to return immediately to Moody and radioed the ground radar operator to announce the alteration.

The radar operator immediately interrupted him and asked whether he had spotted an unusual light in the sky. The operator had been observing the pilot's aerial maneuvers on radar. He reported that when the UFO first appeared on the screen, it was not moving fast enough to be an aircraft. When the F-86 started its climb, the UFO had gotten closer, but afterwards, the other craft had sped up enough to stay just ahead of the fighter. Several minutes later the object accelerated and raced out of range of the jet at an incredibly high speed.

Lamb refused to "swallow those stories" about flying saucers, he told Ruppert, and he determined that he had suffered an attack of vertigo. He was happy he had been alone so that no one else had witnessed his actions.

This encounter, in which a reliable air force pilot had sighted a UFO that was being tracked on radar by army personnel is one of the most credible cases from the early history of the phenomenon. However, Project Blue Book decided that Lamb had "apparently saw the setting planet Venus changing color and shape."

A series of sightings started around Columbus at 7:30 p.m. on Saturday night, March 26, 1966, when Donnie Brown saw an egg-shaped UFO with white and blue lights on the bottom, two lights on the side, and a tail of red-orange flames. "It looked solid," he said.

Several hours later, Bob Fisher, an air traffic controller at Lawson Field, observed an object hovering 2,000 feet above hangars on base. It was thirty-five inches or more in diameter. Initially white, the anomaly shifted colors to light green and sometimes had a red glow. Through binoculars Fisher watched the object swing back and forth like a pendulum, a common UFO maneuver in Georgia at that time.

Fisher alerted Doyle Palmer, an air traffic control operator at Muscogee County Airport, who located a glowing white object that registered on radar and was observed for an hour. The UFO was about six miles southeast of the airport at an altitude of 5,000 feet. Palmer notified Atlanta of the situation, and an air force jet flying between Atlanta and Montgomery was diverted to have a look. The plane combed the area while the two controllers watched the UFO, but the pilot could not visibly locate the anomaly, even though Fisher said the plane was directly over it at one point.

Palmer's UFO was "about the size of a medium flashlight and had a high-intensity light," a newspaper account related. After hovering for an hour, it streaked to a new position and later vanished.

During this time, a police detective observed a glowing, wedge-shaped UFO high in the sky, and three family members saw a disc-shaped object larger than an airplane. A man observed a "flat oval-shaped object" the size of a small airplane that glowed red. It swung like a pendulum, as did another anomaly with two flat sides that spewed a stream of fire. Another fire stream followed an egg-shaped UFO.

At 8 p.m., March 28, Terry Fabian was near Warm Springs Road when he spotted a UFO with glowing red and white lights slowly moving toward Fort Benning. At the same time, brothers Ricky and Bobby Baggett saw a similar object the size of a car that turned sideways before speeding away.

A man and three co-workers were at Lawson Field when they spotted "a bright silver on edge object," a disc, hovering above the base. It suddenly accelerated to a speed of at least 1,000 miles an hour, leaving a white stream behind as it flew west and out of sight. The primary witness was a skeptic and "wouldn't have accepted it as real," if there had been no other witnesses. The encounter lasted ten minutes.

During basic training at Fort Benning, one man's company was receiving nighttime instruction on firing 81 mm mortars. All the men "looked up when this huge saucer-shaped object" floated across the sky. It was silent and had what appeared to be several irregularly-spaced, lighted portholes. The UFO "was spinning in a clockwise rotation about one full turn every two minutes." The object, which resembled a space station a quarter mile in diameter, moved at a speed of about ten miles an hour at an altitude of 500 feet. "A master sergeant was mad at us for looking up," the witness wrote, a reasonable reaction considering they were handling explosive shells.

War of the Worlds

On April 19, 1984, John Vasquez awoke "from a horrific nightmare" about blurry faces. He focused on the faces and realized they were friends from Fort Benning, where he had been stationed as part of Delta Company. While in formation on September 1, 1977, at eight p.m., someone said, "What's that . . . up there?" and pointed to the sky. It was a star that moved precisely, floating back and forth. A sound of rushing wind was followed by a "bright luminous ball of white light" at treetop level and nearing.

Vasquez found the man in front of him entranced, then he faded out and awoke to find himself unable to move. His lower body was paralyzed, and he found other men in the same predicament. When Vasquez called for help, a friend came and picked him up, but shortly he was able to move and joined the exodus.

Men argued about what was occurring, and a sergeant ordered them all to take cover because an aerial object was diving on them. They sought shelter beneath a barracks. A large ball of light disappeared into a building with the sounds of a loud "slap" and a violent "thump."

Loud, high-pitched screaming was heard from the paralyzed men of Alpha, Bravo, Charlie, and Delta companies. Vasquez moved to help them, but a buddy stopped him, saying they were dead. The soldiers then thought they should retrieve their M-16s and ammunition.

Vasquez crawled out from under the building into the intense light and saw a small figure approaching before it faded into the light. It was followed by a large bright light that moved around the building as if searching for something.

Years later, under hypnosis, Vasquez remembered being covered by a blanket and lifted with many others into a "doorway into space" by two beings.

He was in a vast dome that was filled with rows of people laying on floating metal slabs, each receiving a physical exam. When a voice ordered him to sleep, he did. He awoke to a male humanoid telling him to look into its eyes. Those eyes frightened Vasquez. He was told it would be good if he cooperated.

Vasquez did and saw three images as if displayed on a large screen. The first was of himself at a beach peering into a blue sky. The second was terrifying, an image of a planet he thought was earth being destroyed, "followed by eruptions of orange volcanic clouds." The final picture showed an alien humanoid, pasty white, no brows or lashes, small mouth and straight nose, its eyes "like liquid mercury."

Vasquez saw the male again, then awoke in formation at the base, but in a different alignment. His watch had stopped at 7:40. Checking with two other men, he discovered their watches were frozen at 3:30 and 4:45. Back in the barracks soldiers were sick, disoriented, falling down with balance problems.

Vasquez realized that his shirt was buttoned unevenly; the buttons of his pants were also incorrectly aligned. His boot laces were in disarray, and there was a "gooey substance" on his pants. He changed clothes and smelled smoke. Another man thought it was gas and all donned masks and ran outside. When a sergeant asked why they wore the masks, Vasquez told him to take a deep breath. The NCO did and fell over. The men went to each company warning of the gas. That night many men were sick, some had hallucinations, and all suffered nightmares.

In the morning, the men discussed the previous evening, finding none had any memories of it. There was no evidence except for their watches and disarranged clothing. They comforted each other and attempted to explain things as bad dreams.

On the next morning Delta Company left alone to march to a bivouac site, an eight-mile trek while all felt uneasy. After a dispute with a sergeant, all the officers and NCOs left, leaving the recruits alone, which was very unusual.

In the morning, they learned that another company had camped on the other side of their hill and they were equipped with live ammunition, an extremely dangerous situation for a war game. Delta Company selected leaders among themselves and assaulted the other unit, capturing ammo and provisions. On the next night, Green Berets approached and unsuccessfully negotiated for the return of the munitions.

The following night the men fired a flare that burst much brighter than expected. Most were temporarily blinded, and when sight returned Vasquez realized that his awareness was at "a superhuman level." Everyone felt the same.

The unit went to high alert as they thought something was in the trees, and a flare was fired so they could relocate. Then they felt something was wrong as the sky was spinning around. Some panicked and attempted to flee, but they encountered an invisible force field that prevented them from advancing. There was no way through, around, over, or under this shield.

Puzzled, angry, and frightened, they fired a flare and found that as a mass they could push the energy field and move forward. The flares also revealed "shadows," which they realized were exact duplicates of themselves, fifty yards to the rear. The soldiers kept firing flares as they advanced, and one finally "caused a tremendous flash." Normality returned and the shadows disappeared.

The Green Berets appeared and said they had seen the extra 300 soldiers that had instantly disappeared. Vasquez's company again refused to return their ammo.

In the morning, thirty men, including Vasquez, left camp in search of rations. They encountered a shallow body of water and were attacked by a creature as they waded through it. The monster circled ever faster, creating large waves. The men fired at the aquatic anomaly and threw grenades into the water. They escaped, but one man was injured and needed medical assistance.

The thirty men continued to the hospital and left their injured buddy there, locking a security guard in a closet. Outside, they stole two trucks and a jeep and started driving toward their comrades. At two check points Vasquez impersonated a major and convinced lieutenants to allow them to pass.

Back at the bivouac site skirmishing continued between Delta Company and the Green Berets. There was shooting, but no one was hurt and Vasquez arranged a cease fire. He thought it "obvious that someone was trying to get rid of us!"

When a jeep arrived the next afternoon, they stopped it and took a radio. On the radio they heard a news broadcast, "about us!" being transmitted on all military and commercial bands. Delta was declared a danger to military forces and civilians alike. When two additional jeeps arrived, Vasquez's men seized another radio and rations.

When contact was finally made with higher authorities, they were informed that a general was on the way. They would meet him about the ammunition at eight a.m.

The general arrived with an M-60 machine gun aimed at the wayward soldiers, whom the general described as "rebels and renegades." Vasquez asked for trucks to return the men to barracks, a hot meal, and no reprisals for the stolen ammunition. The reluctant general finally agreed, leaving him thinking it was "too easy."

Before returning, Vasquez sent out a scout, who reported tanks and soldiers "surrounding the entire area." His new plan called for them acting pleased with the general's promises while also setting trip flares and quietly marching to the other side of the hill. During the night, the trips flares activated and soldiers fired at their empty tents. A flare revealed their position, so they ran toward the main post and safety. After were being spotted by a helicopter, artillery rounds were fired at them.

Seemingly on the point of destruction, a bright blue-white light neared the copter. Vasquez felt comforted by the light and thought it emitted the message, "Do not be afraid." He ordered the men to enter the light.

They found themselves in a circle facing outward, and saw the aircraft still searching the same area, now about 600 yards away. Three hundred men had been instantaneously transported away from their pursuers. The men ran for their barracks, scaling a ten-foot wall on an obstacle course to escape pursuing blood hounds and reach their destination.

They broke into a supply closet for bedding and the PX for food, went to a medical building to appropriate supplies, and subdued two MPs in a jeep. Vasquez started back to the bivouac, while the other men were captured by the general Vasquez and 140 men reached their starting point, where they ate and rested and were told to relinquish the ammo at six a.m.

They awoke to hot food. Paranoid, they kept some ammo for their rifles. When trucks arrived they forced the drivers to stand aside while they searched the vehicles. The armed soldiers they found were stripped and forced to return to base naked. Vasquez and his men returned to the barracks, where they located the remainder of the company, starving. The mess halls were locked.

They found the barracks booby-trapped and discovered that every soldier at Fort Benning had been removed except for Delta, Charley, Bravo, and Alpha companies. There were no officers or NCOs on base, leaving the soldiers completely unsupervised. The men prepared to organize the base.

After the general and colonel arrived. Vasquez was questioned, and there was talk of mutiny and insubordination. After Vasquez said his actions were unavoidable, the colonel ordered Vasquez to his knees and unholstered his pistol. The general had the colonel arrested and the ammunition was finally exchanged.

Shortly, each company was in formation. It was announced that training would begin again in the morning. The soldiers hoped the odd ordeal was concluded.

The next day went normally, and at six p.m. all were in the barracks. Then, at 10:30 the lights all started to flash, faster until it had a dizzying strobe effect. Alarmed, the men grabbed their M-16s and took formation.

When the general arrived in a jeep, Vasquez explained the situation to him, prompting the general to radio for reserves.

A luminous object approached from 300 yards away. The men were nervous and the general spoke frantically into the radio, summoning a helicopter, which approached the UFO, dropped flares, and fired a missile, which seemed to hit its target, but there was no explosion, just a thump like it had fallen to the ground.

The UFO reacted by brightening and heading for the barracks. The general coordinated a maneuver involving the infantry and a M-60 tank, and Vasquez coordinated with the general and the tank. Two companies were to draw the fire of the UFO, as the alien craft fired "little balls of fire" that traveled rapidly. Men and helicopter returned fire, but the copter was "struck by a large blast of light" and went down. Vasquez and others rescued the crew as a second helicopter arrived to provide cover. Retreating, Vasquez saw a "lot of men lying motionless," looking dead or seriously wounded, but they turned out to be merely unconscious and were carried to shelter.

The general called Green Berets in to assist, with Vasquez working directly under the tank, general, and Green Berets major. They fought for ten minutes, "weapons being fired and men screaming," leaving many wounded.

The major withdrew to regroup. A short battle occurred as the retreat proceeded, soldiers carrying the motionless men with them. Vasquez barely ducked a "small ball of bright light" and returned fire.

He knew he was hitting the target "because the bullets caused a spark that created a small fire when they met with the dark object."

Vasquez dodged another shot, but was hit by a third, which threw him back several feet and knocked him out for nearly an hour. The skin of the wound "turned a bright red with yellow spots" where he was hit.

The wounded all revived, proving that at least the UFO was firing nonlethal rounds.

As a second helicopter circled overhead, a "giant ball of light shot out from the luminous object and completely enveloped" the front of the helicopter. The aircraft fell to ground heavily, bouncing three times without exploding. That crew was also rescued.

The retreat degenerated into chaos, but reinforcements helped to renew the fight. While sheltered beneath a barracks, Vasquez sensed that an alien entity "wanted to talk to me." The general agreed and Vasquez "felt an invisible presence around us." They needed "a method to transfer information," and that came as a telepathic exchange. His mind was "set aside," barely hearing the dialog between alien and general. The experience left him disoriented, and the general seemed startled and pale.

The men returned to barracks for the night, awakening to find everything normal, "even though the night before had been an incredible experience in military combat with an unidentified enemy." The tired men learned that the incident was over. Sergeants and officers said nothing about it, and soldiers never discussed it.

That afternoon a female lieutenant, thought to be a psychiatrist, arrived with burly bodyguards who facilitated her mission to interview every soldier involved. When it was Vasquez's turn he was forced to have an injection and was asked many questions.

He felt they were attempting "to erase everything that I recalled about the strange incident." It would be good to forget the experienced, he was told.

Vasquez wanted to remember, but she told him "to forget everything." The process was painful, and Vasquez thought part of his mind "had been shoved aside."

Afterwards, Vasquez remained on post receiving care for an injured ankle, then had two weeks of leave and was sent to Berlin, where he received a sealed manila envelope and orders to deliver it to Fort Dix, New Jersey, which he did. He believed the secrets of the incident was found within that envelope, but he did not open it. He felt pressured to quickly leave the service and received his discharge.

Vasquez died in 2013 following a car accident.

Some suggest that if these events happened at all, then they might have been a secret psych ops mission involving hallucinogenic drugs.

The morning after his dreams of "blurry faces," Vasquez thought he had hallucinated and saw his doctor, who suggested he research the event, which he did by writing hundreds of letters over the next few years. Despite the fact that he uncovered nothing, about forty percent of *Incident at Fort Benning* consists of "documents" Vasquez gathered. He proved that he was at Fort Benning, but the papers contained absolutely no evidence of any UFO or other strange activity at the base. He argued that the existence of A-10 attack aircraft testing and a measles outbreak were evidence of a vast military cover-up of his experience. Also, Vasquez takes the fact that two helicopters needed repair during the period, admittedly for "superficial" causes, as evidence of the incident. He seemed to believe that a plethora of exclamation marks strengthened his position.

The book reprinted a fraction of the 800 papers he had, and the text said all the "documents" were available from the publisher. I naturally assumed he included his strongest evidence in the book, which proves he had no "proof" of his encounter, although he seemed to believe a lack of documentation constituted evidence.

Vasquez located several men who had been at Fort Benning during that time, but none had memories, or any they were willing to share, of the claimed extraordinary events. He hoped witnesses would come forth after publication of the book.

Vasquez said the aquatic creature was unrelated to the UFO incidents, but proposed that it was a "prehistoric reptile" that may occasionally appear. He also said that two incidents in his account were the result of time warps.

Vasquez thought he and others were not charged with mutiny because the general found the situation untenable. He wanted to get the men from Fort Benning brainwashed and discharged to avoid further problems. The final portion of the book consisted of photographs of himself at Fort Benning, apparently to prove his presence there.

Vasquez admitted that without evidence, his story "will sound like a contrived sci-fi novel."

CORROBORATION OF THE INCIDENT?

Writer and paranormal investigator John Dale Roberts interviewed via telephone a source tagged Ocelot, who claimed to have been a soldier at Fort Benning, but refused to provide information to give his account credence. According to his story, there were six discs, and when the UFOs attacked, the soldiers went to sleep, except for himself and two others, who were taken by a beam into the interior of one of the ships. It was blindingly bright inside, where he could neither move nor speak. He saw three big-headed aliens that he dubbed bug heads, who wore jumpsuits and conversed with a human Man in Black. This was not a UFO attack, but a "joint military-UFO exercise." An implant was placed inside his head, and he had been abducted three additional times by aliens who communicated via telepathy.

Ocelot claimed to have suffered flashbacks for years, but only remembered these encounters four years earlier, when he had been hypnotized by a friend of his wife.

MORE CORROBORATION OF THE INCIDENT?

John Vasquez contacted John Dale Roberts and put him in contact with a former command sergeant major I refer to as CSM. The man was a buck sergeant on September 14, 1977, when he reported for A-10 attack jet exercises with up to 1,300 other men. When live fire started, suddenly there were orbs in the sky, firing lasers through the air.

"Cease fire," was ordered and army helicopters appeared. The aerial orbs changed colors as explosions were heard and a triangle-shaped UFO arrived. Helicopters were destroyed, but their loss was never reported. The base was closed for a time.

After the fighting subsided, two white, unmarked jets arrived to retrieve UFO debris. Apparently, the US Army had won the battle.

The soldiers, who afterward became ill, were told if they revealed the incident that they would be court martialed and sent to prison. As a result of the action, CSM "was burned from a mysterious red substance," had a temperature of 104, and spent two days in a tub of ice water. He suffered missing time and considerable time disorientation. He remembered the incident after being hypnotized.

CSM was currently stationed at Fort McClellan, Alabama, where the army experimented "with biological and chemical substances," and our forces flew UFOs over the facility. He claimed to possess UFO footage, taken with a night-vision device, of a UFO over the base, including one instance when it crossed the horizon in two seconds. Another UFO was a triangle that hovered silently.

CSM claimed to have a piece of a UFO with unintelligible hieroglyphics on it, which he picked up from the crash site at Fort Benning. The material could not be cut or burned and, if bent, returned to its original shape. The item was buried on his property. He promised that all this evidence would be available to UFO researchers and the media.

After CSM's account, Ocelot decided to go public. However, at 5 a.m., as he left for work, "I saw five black sedans parked in front of my house . . . Driving the vehicles were either military men or government men, wearing suits and sunglasses." They left simultaneously, but "continued to stare at me as they drove off."

As a result, Ocelot stated, "I'm OUT . . . I am not going to reveal anything else. I am not going to put my family, my life, in danger . . . the government is NEVER going to reveal" the real Fort Benning story, he declared.

Paul Dale Roberts received word via Facebook that CSM had been detained because of his allegations. He was at the site of the 1977 Incident when, "I was detained by military police," who said "the post commander wanted to talk to me." Instead, his truck was searched, his cell phone taken, and "I was escorted off post." Two vehicles followed him home, and agents told him that the National Security Agency (NSA) wanted to speak to him. Also, "I was told that I better keep my mouth closed or something might happen to me."

On the following day, paranormal radio host Kevin Smith attempted to contact CSM, who returned the call, saying "he had been very busy checking with lawyers to make sure he was 'covered'" before continuing his revelations. When Smith related his fear of CSM being arrested, "he sort of chuckled and said, 'No, I haven't been arrested or nothing like that. They don't have anything to arrest me for. I haven't done nothing to be arrested for.'"

Smith later reported that CSM had been busted from command sergeant major to private and sent "to guard duty at a closed base. On November 13, he was found unconscious at his post and transported to the hospital. He was diagnosed with cancer and Hep C. On November 21, he died in ICU."

But wait, there is still more to this bizarre saga.

Paul Dale Roberts interviewed a man named Bobby Garmon. Many of the details in the interview strongly correlated with statements made by Ocelot. I contacted Roberts and asked if Garmon could be Ocelot. Although Roberts said, "Ocelot could have been Bobby Garmon . . . I can't prove that," he had interviewed both Ocelot and Garmon by telephone and wrote, "The voice was familiar."

Bobby Garmon served in the US Army from 1976 until 2006, in communications. According to the interview with Roberts, in 1977, he was in jump training at Fort Benning with Delta Company when the Incident occurred.

Around 3 a.m. one morning, his unit was in formation when bright lights "that looked like orbs" were seen in the sky and gunfire was heard. A sergeant ordered his men into a building, to a room without windows. As they ran for shelter he saw two helicopters appear in the sky as the gunfire increased and there was a loud explosion.

Garmon later learned what happened from "a guy at the PX," who said they had buried their dog tags there. It was at the PX that Garmon met John Vasquez and they spoke about the encounter.

This interview also made it clear that CSM was James Norton, who was also stationed at Fort Benning at that time. Garmon and Norton had been lifelong friends, having met as boys in Anniston, Alabama. Norton confirmed Garmon's Fort Benning story and said "he was very sick" afterward.

Norton "did tell me he was in danger," Gorman said, but "I did not think much about it at the time."

Interviewer Roberts suggested the MIB (Men in Black) in the SUVs were Military Intelligence (MI). While Roberts served in Military Intelligence they often wore black suits and would not reveal themselves as MI.

Garmon was a witness to the event that apparently killed Norton. Both were stationed at Fort McClellan in northern Alabama. One night when they were pulling guard duty, Norton radioed Garmon to ask if he was being illuminated by Garmon's laser sight.

Garmon said no, but the question intrigued him.

"Then I saw he (Norton) had a bright laser shining on him. I saw a bright light over him, it was a small UFO, but it had lasers lighting his truck. I notified James on the radio/walkie talkie and told him to get out of there," but Norton never responded.

"The UFO moved away over the top of the pine trees very slowly, so I drove down there to where he was, but I could not wake him up, he was out of it, but when he came to he was very sick."

At the hospital Norton was initially told he had a heart attack. He was transferred to a Birmingham hospital accompanied by his sister, who updated Garmon each day.

The doctors "said he was being eaten up with cancer, and then he died the next week from it," leaving Garmon to wonder, "How does a healthy man get cancer instantly and then die from cancer in two weeks?"

The same beam "burned my shoulder," Garmon stated, adding that the "incident scared the hell out of me."

At Fort McClellan Garmon said he and Norton "saw many UFOS, one huge, one as big as a football field (that) would come from the northeast and move very slowly across the sky, but it would . . . vanish in a blink of your eye. It would be gone only to show in a second."

The men "were told never to talk about it, even to each other. James tried to get me to tell what happened, but I would not talk about it at that time."

AN EARLIER INCIDENT?

On November 17, 2009, Kenneth Darnell related a Fort Benning UFO encounter that occurred in the spring of 1977, which he thought might have a correlation in time to the Vasquez episode.

Darnell, fifty-one, had a long career as a correctional training specialist, and lived in North Carolina with his family.

After basic training at Fort Knox, Kentucky, at the age of eighteen, Darnell arrived at Fort Benning in January 1977, for parachute training and indirect fire infantry school. His UFO experience came in March or April, his "memory quite clear" and "never forgotten . . . I know what I witnessed that night was not of this world."

That night his platoon was in line to collect their laundry for the week. As they stood, he noticed several of his comrades looking up and pointing toward the sky. Darnell followed their gaze and saw eight to twelve "points of light, white and silent and larger than stars." Those lights moved like "a swarm of gnats" around each other. Suddenly, one light grew brighter and larger than the others, and as abruptly, those "other 'swarming' lights suddenly formed a perfect circle around the brighter light and began to slowly rotate around it. The brighter light suddenly left the circle at tremendous speed and shot across the sky and suddenly stopped."

The bigger light became alternately brighter and dimmer, and "did several movements, always at tremendous speed, sometimes making abrupt 90-degree turns, moving from horizon to horizon. Then it suddenly sped back and suddenly stopped in the circle of smaller rotating lights."

The larger light dimmed to the size of the others, and all began to "swarm" again. Then the entire ballet began again. One light brightened, was circled by the others, raced to perform various maneuvers, all much "faster than any human-produced craft could travel." The cycle was repeated several times. Suddenly, the entire fleet disappeared.

Darnell was left frightened, understanding that humans could not have performed those maneuvers, and the laws of physics "would not allow such speed, sudden stops, or abrupt turns."

Darnell had always wondered why such an incident, witnessed by so many, was not investigated by base security or reported in the media.

A Mini Incident?

A report to the National UFO Reporting Center (NUFORC) claimed another UFO invasion at Fort Benning at midnight on August 16, 1968, nine years before Vasquez's account. Contact was lost with a restricted compound when three silent, "dull yellow glowing orbs" hovered 1,500 feet above the facility, which had lost power (the only building so affected). Radios ceased operating, and all the personnel were found asleep. His unit was "placed on full alert, issued weapons, and munitions." The UFOs departed in a "slow vertical ascent." The soldiers met with the "base top brass," who told them, "no report will be made," and that they would remain silent or "we would be tried under official secrets act." For years afterwards, the man was "afraid to say more."

Bigfoot Skinny Dipping

Terry grew up in rural Georgia, in the Fort Benning area. In 1982, he and his girlfriend were returning from their high school prom when they spotted a ten-foot-tall Bigfoot standing alongside the highway. The creature was massive, with rippling muscles and shiny black fur.

At another time that year, Terry wrote on the Georgia Bigfoot Society's website that he, his girlfriend, and her father were parked on Fort Benning property two feet from the banks of the Chattahoochee River, headlights blazing across the water. The father was "night cat fishing," sitting on the car's hood with his fishing pole while the young couple sat in the front seat conversing.

Suddenly, to his right, "I heard the most horribly incredible scream." Sixty feet in that direction the undergrowth was extremely "swampy, very thick and very hard to walk through."

Upon hearing the sound, Terry went into shock. As he slowly turned to the right, he heard two additional loud noises. The first "sounded like a huge branch shaking like someone jumping off into the water. The splash that came next was equally horrific."

The three people didn't move, they just sat staring at the water until "a huge black object, about nine feet long/tall floated into view of our headlights and stopped," apparently a deliberate act as it was floating downstream. After what seemed like hours, "it opened its eyes (two huge balls of red light)" reflecting the car's headlights.

The father leaped into the driver's seat, slammed the car into reverse, "and we sped off extremely terrified."

After Terry retired from the US Navy, he earned a degree in business administration and started working for a company in California in high speed data management.

FORT GILLEM

This military installation, located in the southern portion of metropolitan Atlanta, seems innocuous enough. Founded in 1941 as the Atlanta Army Depot, a sub-post of Fort McPherson, it trained troops and processed supplies for the military from World War II through Vietnam. In 1973, the 1,465-acre area, containing numerous large warehouses, was annexed by the city of Forest Park.

The closing of Fort Gillem was announced in 1975, and much of the army personnel was transferred in 2011. After years of negotiation, the city of Forest Park purchased most of the property for thirty million dollars and hopes to develop it for industry, manufacturing, warehouses, and other businesses. The army retained 250 acres for the US Army Criminal Investigations Crime Laboratory, which is a forensic crime lab, and the 3rd MP Group.

The Mystery: Paranoid and Delusional

For some unknown reason (but then urban legends do not need reason), the story (and mystery) got around that when the "government take-over" occurs, that thousands of prisoners would be held here as a FEMA designated detention facility.

FORT GORDON

Located near Augusta, Fort Gordon was established in 1917, beginning its specialization in training Signal Corps personnel for World War I. Reconstructed in 1941, the facility trained three divisions, the 4th and 26th Infantry, and the 10th Armored. Postwar, in addition to Signal Corps, Fort Gordon became the army's military police school.

Signals continues to be the most important aspect of the installation, which hosts the US Army Cyber Command, working with both military and civilian intelligence assets, including the National Security Agency. There are 30,000 military and civilian workers at Fort Gordon.

Ghosts

Rhondaskppr moved with her husband and daughter to Fort Gordon in December 2006; a son was soon born. One day the couple met at the hospital for their son's shots. He returned to work and she went home. As she unlocked the front door, her three-year-old daughter looked through a window and asked, "Who's that man?"

"What, honey?" Mom inquired, peeking herself to make certain there wasn't an intruder waiting inside. "I don't see anyone, Sweetie." But the child insisted, "He's right there. I thought Daddy went back to work."

"He did," Mom said. "His car isn't here."

Inside the child said, "Well, he's gone now."

When Rhondaskppr asked for a description of the man, the child replied, "He had on a uniform like Daddy wears."

"Right then I knew we had a ghost/spirit," Rhondaskppr wrote to *Your Ghost Stories*.

The daughter was unconcerned and started playing a Dora the Explorer video game on TV while her mother started ironing her husband's uniforms. Mom "felt a

Ghosts are thought to haunt soldier's housing at Fort Gordon.

really cold chill" and her daughter said again, "Mommy, who is that man?" When Mom asked about it, the girl said he was gone.

Mom and daughter stepped outside and Mom asked if the man scared or said anything to her. The daughter simply said, "No."

After the kids were in bed that night, Rhondaskppr told her husband about the incident. He didn't want to hear about ghosts, resulting in "a huge fight." He settled down in front of the TV while she went to bed.

Hubby came home for lunch the following day and apologized for his behavior. He said that as "he was making his way to bed the night before, the bathroom door opened and something black was standing there. It didn't say anything, but he got a really strong feeling that the spirit didn't like him fighting with me."

Rhondaskppr thought it was funny, "because I know how ghosts can feed off negative energy," but felt this ghost didn't want the conflict. However, "I know he's still here because if my husband fights with me, I can tell something freaks him out."

A friend of her husband's came for a visit and they didn't like that he brought a girlfriend with him. As the couple tried to sleep upstairs, Rhondaskppr asked her husband to go down, "and tell them to keep the noise down. I was angry because he was disrespecting our home."

Suddenly, a "loud breaking noise" was heard and both raced downstairs to find, "all of my makeup over the floor all the way to the bottom of the stairs," which was a distance.

When Rhondaskppr and husband demanded an explanation from the friend and lover, "They looked like they were scared out of their minds," and were unable to speak. Husband shook the visitor, and the friend said, "Dude, we didn't do that, we haven't moved from the couch."

The visitors left immediately. The husband walked him out and returned to tell Rhondaskppr, "my boy just told me we have a ghost. I guess they made our ghost mad, too." The husband explained that the ghost "only lets us know he's here if we fight and now we know he doesn't like anyone disrespecting our home."

That ended the paranormal activity in the house, "but everyone knows not to act stupid in our home," Rhondaskppr concluded.

Bigfoot

In December 1979, Jack Hovatter was hunting with his son in the woods of Fort Gordon. At the Small Arms Impact Area, he saw the faint impression of a footprint on the hard ground of a ravine. He thought it was the front and back feet of a bear, but his son looked at it from a different angle and said, "No Dad, that's one track," Hovatter told Wayne Ford of the *Athens Banner Herald* in 2003. His son thought it humanlike and flat-footed. Using his shotgun as a measuring stick, Hovatter calculated it was twenty-two inches long and nine inches in width at the ball of the foot. This was a preamble to the most frightening moments in Hovatter's life.

Nearby were about twenty to thirty large piles that seemed like ant hills. "We dug down to the bottom, but it was just sand piled on the ground," he said, "like a three- or four-gallon bucket was dumped" to form each pile.

Father and son left, but the print intrigued Hovatter, who returned alone about a week later for a closer examination of the area. He found that the ravine was created by a spring-fed stream, the center of three waterways that formed the headwaters of South Prong Creek. The floor of the ravine was flat and open, except for a few small trees, and around the stream was what appeared to be an impenetrable thicket, a "tight ring of brush" beyond the sand piles. Looking closer, he found a narrow gap and trail and followed it inside the thicket.

"I get inside," a distance of about twelve feet, where "I heard something coming toward me." Suddenly, "here that thing came. It's not like it was trying to catch me. It was trying to scare me," and he "didn't like the look on its face."

The "thing" was an enormous, hairy, ape-like creature on two feet that measured about ten feet in height. Hovatter was awed by its height and the width of the shoulders, about five feet across. Comparing it to horses and cows, "I'd say it weighed at least 1,000 pounds," or more. "Its arms were massive," longer than a human's. The creature "was all big-boned muscle, no body fat." He "didn't see any ears and its hair was kind of short, almost like a hound dog. It didn't have any hair around its eyes, or its mouth or its nose." The hair was an inch in length, dark brown to black, "but with a salt and pepper look." The legs were massive, with toes that "went on an angle but evenly straight in line."

The Bigfoot had "dark deep-set eyes, the head sloped back and was Neanderthal shaped, had no eyebrows," he told the Bigfoot Field Researchers Organization (BFRO), Case # 2218. There were "prominent lips but not protruding, jutting square chin, no ears or teeth were seen, prominent nostrils, slight nose (not flat like a gorilla), and an aged look to the face." The creature made no sound, nor was a smell detectable.

This was one of the largest Bigfoot creatures ever witnessed, and it had obviously managed to achieve a stable lifestyle in a sustainable habitat and achieved considerable maturity.

"I wanted to turn and run," Hovatter said, "but I've always heard that with a wild animal that's a bad thing to do. I had a shotgun, but (the creature) was too big and too close. It seems like a 16-gauge shotgun is a powerful weapon until I saw something that big, that close up. It felt like I had a .22." Later, he said the shotgun "might as well have been a pellet gun." The firearm was a semi-automatic loaded with slugs, but he immediately rejected the idea of using it on the animal, a common occurrence in the presence of an intimidating Bigfoot.

Hovatter backed away slowly down the path, and felt great relief that the creature "did not pursue me." Although frightened by the encounter, he found the animal "not especially threatening," believing it had taken "more like a positive defensive move."

As Hovatter exited, he swung around the ravine to cut back on the terror, and detected the strong smell of vomit. He discovered its source, "a big pile of vomit," with a volume of approximately three gallons. "I took a stick and investigated it, and it had a piece of deer skin in there that was about two feet square." Most of the pile consisted of "poorly digested acorns."

Near the vomit was a hillock of stool containing "deer skin, acorns, and tree bark." A nearby tree was stripped of its bark to "a height of eight to ten feet."

Apparently, Bigfoot had eaten something that had not agreed with him and threw up the contents of its enormous stomach. The refuse proved that it would gobble any available food.

"I went right up to the head of the ravine . . . and back to my truck," Hovatter told Eric Johnson of the Augusta *Metro Spirit* in 2010. "Lord, was I glad to get back into my truck."

Hovatter shared his shocking story with a brother in Tennessee, who contacted an official in a natural resources organization. This third person obtained permission from Fort Gordon to investigate, but the ravine had been leveled by bulldozers, the thicket destroyed.

Hovatter, retired from the army, still lives in Augusta.

BFRO Case # 4263

In June 1965, Henry was a fourteen-year-old high school student whose father was a "military NCO Basic Training Instructor" at Fort Gordon. Although new housing was being constructed on base for NCOs and officers, his family lived in a former barracks converted into four family apartments. In the area were other converted barracks, dense pine woods, and old infantry training fields that were overgrown with tall weeds.

A girl in an apartment below his told him that "her little brother would tell her that a big man would look through their window at night." This seemed unlikely because the window started at a height of seven to eight feet from ground level. Henry dismissed the story and forgot about it.

During the long summer vacation, Henry and friends spent time in the woods stalking wildlife.

"We would go downwind and get as close to deer as possible just to take a photo or observe the animals without disturbing them."

One day, none of his friends were around, so Henry went alone. He walked down a slope and 200 yards to the edge of the woods. Bulldozers were preparing an area for new officers' quarters, and in the exposed clay, he found "some big footsteps" that extended into the woods. They "were so enormous that I began to observe them." The prints appeared to be human, with five toes, but measured eighteen inches in length and five inches in width.

Henry took a trail into the woods and soon noticed, "I did not hear birds nor did I see any squirrels." All he heard was the wind blowing tree branches about, "but no sign of life in the area." He got "goose bumps as if someone or something was watching all my moves."

The youngster sat on a rock to observe his surroundings. Soon, "I started to hear some heavy bipedal footsteps in the grass and leaves," about fifty feet from him. The grass and underbrush was so thick that he could only see twenty feet. He was suddenly overwhelmed by "my human nature or animal instincts," and decided to vacate, cautiously at first, but then, "I steadily began to work out of the wood and as I did, I could hear the heavy bipedal footsteps stalking me from the left, deeper in the woods from where I was at. If I stopped walking, it would stop walking. If I ran a little, it would run a little," and it paused a few seconds after he did.

As Henry neared the edge of the woods his shadower "began to run very fast coming towards me. I then thought it was time to run like hell. I picked up a running speed that surprised me," and only stopped, out of breath, on his front porch.

A friend had seen the end of the run and asked what happened. When the friend refused to believe his story, Henry challenged him to see if the creature was still there. The boy accepted, and when shown the big footprints, declared it "the Bigfoot monster." Henry had never heard of such, saying "it must be some big hillbilly or hobo person living in the area that does not want us to disturb him."

The boys perched on the same rock occupied earlier by Henry. Soon they felt as if they were being watched and the forest sounds disappeared. "Suddenly, the heavy bipedal footsteps once again began to stalk us in the brush," as it had earlier. When the boys walked, the stalker walked; when the boys stopped, the stalker paused. The skin of Henry's friend nearly turned "tomato red. I knew he was more afraid that I was at that moment."

Abruptly, "the heavy footsteps began to run towards us. We could near the brush breaking and moving," and both boys sprinted for home. On the porch they slowly began to get their breath back. The friend said that "he had seen something big that moved in the brush. He was not certain what it was."

Today Henry acknowledges that he encountered Bigfoot. BFRO investigator Matt Pruitt interviewed Henry and found his amount of detail "highly impressive." He also believes "that the animal encountered that day was indeed a Sasquatch."

UFOs

Fort Gordon, home to the US Army Signal Corps, would be expected to be observed by other countries, or worlds, and is. At 10 p.m. on April 17, 1977, a young man reported to NUFORC, that he had been standing guard with another soldier when he noticed a fireball. After he "reported it to my drill sergeant, he thought I was a lunatic."

Ten minutes later the soldier saw another aerial mystery—an object brighter than a halogen light at a height of thirty feet, "stealthily coming above me. It would stop directly over my head, as if it were observing me, and I would stand there just looking back at it. Originally, it had lights on, and I stood there just looking and thinking. I was armed, and never once did I think of shooting at the object. For me it was as if time had stood still . . . The object turned its lights off and stayed hovering above the trees and me for a few more seconds and then it just suddenly took off at a speed unimaginable."

Quite an unnerving experience.

In January 2000, Robert McPhalan informed Paranormal.about.com that he was one of about thirty soldiers who gathered nightly for training at a secure facility. A white bus carried them to a large field, where they waited for an NCO to unlock a gate in a twenty-foot-high fence, topped with razor wire. Once they were inside, that gate was locked and a second twenty-foot-high gate, with its own razor wire, was unlocked to admit them to the facility.

This was their normal routine. The area had many "large, ominous signs stating that we couldn't talk about, take pictures of, draw, or record anything in this area." They had also signed nondisclosure agreements, swearing, "we couldn't talk about the equipment we'd be working on." However, he noted, "it didn't say anything about stuff we saw in the sky."

After three hours training one night, McPhalen heard a soldier shout, "Look at that @$%# UFO!" He did look up and "saw an incredibly bright, very large light moving across the sky!" Within a second the soundless object was gone.

Afterwards, other men would not talk about it, and the initial witness claimed it had been a weather balloon. McPhalen immediately dismissed that claim; he was familiar with weather balloons, "and they certainly don't race across the sky." After this incident he found himself scanning the sky for hours.

In November 2000, a soldier returned to the barracks after dinner and found two men who claimed to have seen a UFO. Although they had been drinking, he humored them.

"They claimed to have seen three reddish-orange lights appear in a triangular formation and a fourth a little ways off that flew around the [clear, dark] sky, and then faded out of sight."

As they talked, one of them pointed into the air at a light that had appeared. It was stationary for ten seconds, then faded away. Two minutes, later, "four lights appeared, three in a line and one lower to the right. As I watched, the furthest right light in the line faded out, just as a fifth light appeared on the left, almost as if a giant cylindrical object was slowly turning. After fifteen minutes or so, this display faded out completely."

Two other soldiers had now joined the party. About every two minutes one light appeared at least three times. Of most concern, the UFOs, "were possibly overhead of the new NSA expansion being constructed on post."

The witness who reported this sighting to NUFORC was a twenty-two-year-old intelligence analyst. He considered himself "highly skeptical about aliens but willing to admit that this was a flying object I could not identify." He also thought it could have been a "weird training exercise."

Linda observed a unique UFO manifestation that occurred just above the tree line along the border of Fort Gordon, between Gates 1 and 2. It was 7:40 p.m. on December 12, 2013, when she stepped "outside and noticed a bright, white light." Linda thought it was a plane, and when two similar lights appeared, she feared an imminent midair collision would occur.

At that point the three UFOs faded out but were replaced by a dozen more. These "lights all kept fading in and out. As soon as one faded in, another faded out."

The lights were not aligned, but more like "a scattered zigzag" and the number varied considerably. As one would fade out, two or three would appear, all slowly moving north.

After three minutes, one UFO expanded considerably and turned bright orange, then faded away. One by one, two others went orange as the others continued fading in and out.

When two UFOs left the rest and started toward Linda's house, she ran inside and locked the doors, "scared and shaking." Two minutes later, she peered out a window and saw two remaining lights. Following three additional minutes, she heard a helicopter, presumably from Fort Gordon, that circled the area for five minutes, apparently searching for the UFO, but found nothing.

The Mutual UFO Network (MUFON) reported an incident that occurred at 1:55 a.m. seven days later. A man was driving toward the hunting area on base and glanced up to determine the location of the moon, "when I noticed a bright orb hovering over the NSA complex." After hovering for a while, the sphere "descended straight down and vanished."

FORT MCPHERSON

Located in East Point, this area of southwestern Atlanta has been used for military purposes since 1835, including by Confederate troops during the Civil War and federal occupation forces during Reconstruction. The US Army established a post here in 1885 with McPherson Barracks. During World War I, McPherson trained American troops and was a prison for German prisoners of war. Closure of the 487-acre base was announced in 2005 and accomplished in 2011. The city of Atlanta acquired the property for development as housing, a research park, and mixed use. Forty acres comprise a historical district.

UFOs

A declassified Blue Book document, dated July 10, 1950, and released in 1962, was titled, "Unidentified Object Sighted over Fort McPherson, Georgia." The small UFO, described as "a metallic object" seen high in the air, had a "bright metallic appearance." It was observed by three members of the 111th CIC Detachment, including a major, for fifteen minutes, moving east at a very slow speed until obscured by clouds.

In 1964, a man lived in East Point in a "community of mostly military families stationed at Ft. Mac." Looking at the sky toward the military installation, he saw "this formation of oval-shaped one-dimensional lights." Initially, he thought they were advertising lights for a car dealership, but then the UFOs slowed and stopped, then "disappeared by speeding sideways."

The witness speculated that the operation had been conducted by time travelers, "extraterrestrials from another galaxy," or was the Soviet Union provoking a "Cold War showdown."

FORT SCREVEN

The important port of Savannah has been protected by fortifications constructed on Tybee Island for hundreds of years. When the Spanish-American War started in 1898, the Savannah River was virtually undefended. Quickly, a series of defenses known as Endicott batteries were erected, stout concrete gun positions hunkered down behind sand dunes. Twelve-inch rifled artillery, firing 600-pound shells propelled by 200-pound bags of powder to a distance of ten miles, were raised to fire, then recoil brought them back down to be reloaded.

Paranormal activity has been witnessed around the old coastal fortifications of Fort Screven on Tybee Island.

BATTERY GARLAND
1899
FORT SCREVEN

TYBEE ISLAND
MUSEUM
BATTERY GARLAND
1899
OPERATED BY THE TYBEE ISLAND
HISTORICAL SOCIETY

These batteries were decommissioned in 1942 and sold to the town of Tybee Island five years later. Battery Garland was converted into the Tybee Island Museum. Other batteries, nearly indestructible, were converted to clubs and unique homes. Most sit empty, still facing the Atlantic Ocean.

Ghosts

OffDutyCop (ODC) traded in plainclothes detective work to return to uniformed patrolling and accepted a job with the Tybee Island Police Department. Tybee is largely a vacation destination near Savannah.

"So far," he wrote, "I've greatly enjoyed the sun, sand, ocean air, and general relaxed feel of our quirky little town."

At 3 a.m. on August 4, 2010, ODC was on patrol in the Fort Screven Historic District. As he reached the Tybee Island Museum in Battery Garland, he saw a car in the parking lot. What concerned him was that several feet from the car, "I observed a round ball of bright light," which looked like a flashlight held "at approximately head level for a person of average height, reminding me of the way police officers, or security guards, tend to hold a flashlight just above their shoulder, next to their heads." This type of light could also be a common paranormal phenomenon known as a "ghost light."

ODC called his supervisor to ask if the museum had night security or if someone was supposed to be there at that late hour. Receiving a negative response, he pulled into the lot, noting "that the light was now gone, and that I had not seen anyone in, or around, the area." The parked vehicle was secure, and he informed his superior that he would walk around the building, "checking doors and windows."

ODC circled the building and found his superior parked in the lot near his own patrol car. Before conferring, he "decided to stop, turn around, and look for anything that I may have mistaken for a flashlight." He found nothing. Upon reaching his superior, he thought the officer looked "'uneasy', and immediately asked me if I had gotten 'spooked.'"

ODC said he was just checking the area, and his superior "continued to act a bit nervous, before telling me, 'This place is haunted.'"

ODC laughed, thinking it might be a joke, and said he would finish checking the museum's exterior. However, "instead of joining me, as officers usually do, he drove his car to the other end of the parking lot, putting as much distance between himself and the fort as possible, and parked."

When the patrolman returned, the supervisor "simply looked at me and said, 'I'm telling you, this place is haunted,' then drove away."

Intrigued, ODC spoke to residents of the district, "and all agreed it was haunted, some sharing personal experiences, and others simply passing on things they had heard over the years."

007

FORT STEWART AND HUNTER ARMY AIRFIELD

Fort Stewart originated in 1940 as an ant-iaircraft training center during World War II; it contained two POW camps for captured Axis soldiers. Schools for cooks, bakers, and postal personnel followed. By 1944, the base held 55,000 soldiers, most of whom participated in the invasion of France.

Postwar the base was reduced to twenty-two military and fifty civilian workers. During Korea, anti-aircraft training returned with basic training and the addition of armor. In 1959, Fort Stewart became a center for armor and field artillery. When the Cuban Missile Crisis developed, the 1st Armored Division, 30,000 soldiers strong, arrived and was visited in November 1962 by President John F. Kennedy.

Vietnam brought training for helicopters. The acquisition of Hunter Army Airfield from the air force in 1967 attracted the US Army Flight Center and America's largest Coast Guard unit.

In 1974, the 24th Infantry Division was based at Stewart, becoming mechanized in 1980. When Iraq invaded Kuwait in 1990, the division's vehicles and equipment were shipped from the deep water port of Savannah, while the soldiers flew out of Hunter. Within a month the division was in the Middle East fighting in Desert Storm.

In 1996, the 24th was deactivated and the 3rd Infantry Division activated at Fort Stewart. Tank, artillery, helicopter, and small arms training occurs daily.

The Fort Stewart Museum is undergoing a major renovation with no estimated date of completion.

Ghosts

When the Army acquired the vast area for Fort Stewart, entire communities ceased to exist, and more than sixty cemeteries of various sizes were annexed. The cemeteries are maintained by the army.

Bragg Cemetery dates to the Civil War. While passing it one day, Desirae and her husband saw "a man standing outside the cemetery in old-looking clothes." When they passed, "he disappeared." A week later Desirae told her husband that she had to return to the cemetery to investigate.

When they opened the gate, "I got a really cold chill throughout my body and we both heard a strange noise like a child crying," she said, but there was not a child within miles of the cemetery.

At the first grave, the "crying and whimpering got louder and louder . . . The noise sounded as if it was coming from the corner of the cemetery." At that point they hurriedly departed the grounds.

Within five minutes, "my husband had a burning feeling on his neck—just one spot was really red and extremely warm." By the next day, it was swollen, red, and had "six little black dots in a circle right below his ear." In conclusion, they were "still not sure what that was from," she informed HauntedHovel's website.

Desirae's husband related several Fort Stewart paranormal stories to her, including a ghost soldier who was "known to kind of protect one of the cemeteries." Late one night her husband and two friends visited one graveyard, where they saw "a soldier dressed in old gear . . . from the Civil War walking along the graves."

As one soldier leaned against a grave marker, "the soldier had started walking straight towards him pretty quickly." Another of the three knelt to examine a tombstone, "and all of a sudden the soldier was right next to him, kneeling down, just staring at him."

Fort Stewart soldiers also recorded ghost tales on *Ghosts of America*. Seth broke his leg during PT in 2007. As part of his therapy, he walked and jogged on the tank trail near the TF Building. One night he was walking the trail with half a dozen other injured soldiers. They went right at the "Y" intersection and passed a pond to come out near the fort entrance at the AAFE gas station.

The men were passing one of three old cemeteries along the trail, when "all witnessed an apparition kneeling in one of the cemeteries." The ghost was glowing and "once we drew closer to him, he stood, looked at us as if attempting to determine if we were a threat, turned his back on us, and vanished."

"In the hospital, there have been many sightings of an old surgeon wandering the halls," reported 91. "He is known to turn on medical equipment. I personally saw him turn on the washer/sterilizer in the basement of the hospital."

There seem to be different soldier ghosts haunting different areas. One named Lancaster was killed in Vietnam and always appeared headless, Ray reported. A friend and one of his buddies told him they had seen it. Ray thought the spirit "had something going on about Fort Stewart." He didn't understand why ghosts frequent particular places, but wished luck to anyone stationed there.

In November 2006, Alan was a medic stationed at Fort Stewart and living in a two-man room. One of his treasured possessions was a Leatherman, a multi-knife and tool, always handy for a soldier. The Leatherman disappeared for a week, then reappeared during cleaning. Alan put the tool away in a drawer of his locked closet. He had started folding laundry, when "all of sudden (it) came flying in front of my field of vision," as "if it had been thrown." His roomie had been in the bathroom. The incident left him "unnerved." He returned the Leatherman to the locked closet.

Five minutes after Alan and his roommate turned off the lights and went to bed, "we heard a thud and a clatter," Alan wrote. With the lights on, the roommates found the Leatherman on the floor. Both were a little spooked, so Alan decided to throw the thing away, "literally. I went outside and tossed it until it hit the other barracks." When Alan returned to his room "my aid bag came crashing down inside my closet."

In response, the roommates enlisted a friend, who would spend the night in their room. The three searched for and retrieved the Leatherman, and they had two duty soldiers lock it inside the office. By morning, the tool had vanished again and never returned.

Alan had picked up the knife from an airborne drop zone. He noted that accidents occasionally occurred, and "deaths happen when you are jumping out of a plane." He wondered if that could be the cause of the haunting.

Plus, there were other "odd things occurring in my room. Last night there were DVD cases that were being moved about, a PlayStation that was turned off was turned back on by itself, odd noises that we could not identify and such."

Alan and the roommate believed their "room was haunted."

One day Miles was standing near some trees, where he "heard a dog barking. I looked up to see a medium-sized dark brown dog running toward me with his teeth bared as if he was going to attack me. The dog leaped into the air to jump on me . . . and then vanished completely." Miles stood still for several minutes, waiting for his heart to pound "out of my chest." Just thinking about it gave him goosebumps, and he believes in the existence of ghost dogs. The military uses many canines, and some are buried on post.

Walter, who once lived at Fort Stewart, knew "there were many strange things that happened and many strange things that were seen by people."

He believed military personnel "just shrug things off and keep their mouths shut," but he knew that they could not erase such events from their memories. "I wish I could forget about the things I saw while living there." He also wished luck to those stationed in the area, because they would need it.

UFOs

It was 1962 or 1963, and the witness reporting this encounter to NUFORC was nine or ten. It was a Saturday, and the boy's family had been shopping in Savannah, returning with a helium-filled Mickey Mouse balloon, which was the envy of the neighborhood. It was about 9:30 p.m., and the boy, his brothers, and other kids played a game with Mickey. They ripped up pieces of paper, placed them between Mickey's ears, and let the balloon float, secured with kite string, above the street lights. At that point the string was jerked vigorously, and as the paper floated down, the boys raced to collect them. The child with the most pieces won.

On round two or three, "a luminous disk about the size of a car suddenly appeared and then zig-zagged half a dozen times above the street light, first side to side, then back and forth in a cross-like pattern alternating aggressively," apparently while scrutinizing the balloon. Every kid was transfixed by the UFO, and the papers floated to earth unnoticed. Then, "as suddenly as it appeared, it disappeared."

The boys scrambled to collect the paper, hoisted Mickey again, and jerked the string, "and almost the exact same thing happened again," except instead of disappearing, the UFO "took off in a straight line," slow enough that they could track it.

The UFO had been silent and all the kids saw of it was the bottom. It was described as "incredibly zippy" and "glowing silvery-amber." By the time adults were summoned, the UFO was lost among the stars.

In October 1983, Ian was a security specialist MP with the 24th Infantry Division. His unit had spent weeks in the field, training for an exercise called Desert Sting, in California. Already looking forward to some well-earned rest, he was dismayed by one more drill, this one an air attack. The jeeps screeched to a halt and the men bailed out to aim their weapons at the sky. On his back, Ian thought it was "a fantastic night." Climbing back aboard the jeep, he "saw three objects that looked like the stars around them. They performed perfect circles in the sky, same altitude, same speed, same spacing. It was perfection . . . I felt in awe." It was difficult for him to find the right words to describe the aerial ballet he had witnessed.

A BORG CUBE?

According to *UFOEvidence*, in July 1988, a tank crewman with the 1/64th armor was on a field training exercise in the swamps. They had established a defensive position for the night and were sitting on top of their M-1 Abrams Main Battle Tank, when the four-man crew witnessed an "extremely large square or cube," silent, with "ten–fifteen very bright colored lights."

The UFO "flew directly above my platoon, and was followed by army helicopters a few minutes later." The cube, one hundred feet to a side, "had beautiful colored lights that were as bright as stadium lights," and traveled just 200 feet above the ground. "It was too large to remain airborne without an engine, yet flew by at a brisk speed." His lieutenant joked, "I didn't see anything," indicating that this incident would not be reported.

The witness, a resident of Roseburg, Oregon, did not believe in UFOs; he just didn't "know what the heck it was." He wrote that it was "obviously made by man or some being." He was then thirty-nine years old, a police officer with two BS degrees.

MUFON CASE # 42566

It was August 1988, 9 p.m., according to the report, and the witness was a member of the Georgia Army National Guard. One night, during their annual training, his tank battalion was at a live fire range. They were twenty miles away from the main post, observing light discipline, so it was very dark, the stars clearly visible. The witness was looking for shooting stars when he spotted a light at 160 degrees. The UFO, a single bright light without shape, was silent and too high to be a plane. After he called fifteen other men's attention to it, they speculated about what it could be. Suddenly, "it shot halfway across the sky in the blink of an eye," and "all knew it was not a worldly craft." For fifteen minutes, "we watched it zigzag every two to three minutes all over the sky." They thought "it looked like a continuous shooting star," silent and too distant to determine a shape

Another member of the Georgia Army National Guard submitted a report to NUFORC, his sighting taking place at night in February 1989. He was a COMSEC officer, part of the 1/230 Field Artillery Battalion, in the Observation Point during an artillery firing exercise. With him were forward observers and a number of active duty evaluators. It was a clear winter night, with no moon light.

One man at the OP saw the object and drew everyone's attention to it. The UFO, looking like a small star, "just kept moving in very bizarre movements. It zigged and zagged, but it seemed to stay overhead." Considering their position at an important military base, they thought "it (a) spy satellite," which "seemed to be looking at us." However, its "movements were so unusual that we had to call it a UFO."

In late March 2004, at 10 p.m., a soldier was talking to his family on his cell phone near the barracks. Overhead he "saw a bright object falling from the sky," at a forty-five-degree angle and a high rate of speed, he informed *UFOstalker.com*. He estimated it was twenty to thirty miles away.

"The object seemed to have two explosions during its descent," and disappeared following the last blast. He did not believe the explosions were the result of an aircraft dispensing chaff, artillery fire, airplane fire, or fireworks. "The explosions came from the object and were bright enough to be seen in the sky," despite the lights of a nearby festival. He also thought "it did not have the usual characteristics of a falling star."

According to UFO-hunter.com, it was the evening of September 23, 2007, when a man and his buddy saw "some strange moving lights" above the treetops at a distance. Initially, they thought it was the helicopters they often saw flying across Fort Stewart. The lights moved up and down before approaching them. When they saw "lights that appeared to revolve or shift around the object," they realized it wasn't a chopper. The UFO drew closer and hovered above a house across the street, then disappeared.

Bigfoot

Fort Stewart, located north of Savannah and thirty miles east of the Atlantic Ocean, is a 280,000-acre training base for armor, the largest facility east of the Mississippi River. The base is thirty-nine miles east to west, and nineteen miles north to south, occupying portions of five Georgia counties. Much of the military installation consists of swamp and piney woods, a perfect habitat for many animals, including Bigfoot.

BFRO CASE # 4109

At dusk one day in December 1995, Army Sgt. RB, two other squad leaders, and two privates started out on a reconnaissance mission to locate a second unit stationed several miles away. They were at Fort Stewart's western perimeter, a roadless, uninhabited, and remote part of the enormous military reservation, an area with deep swamp and some higher ground covered with pine trees. There was a full moon, and despite mist, visibility was good.

Consulting a map and compass, the group decided to advance through several hundred meters of swamp, believing that no one would expect them to take that route. They exited the swamp at 11 p.m., within forty yards of the fort's border, a mile distant from the opposing force.

After leaving the swamp, "we could hear something or someone following us," Sgt. RB wrote. They considered it could be their instructors, but concluded they would not have taken the swamp route, and no one knew their path.

"Although we didn't see it, it was easily within twenty-five yards. It would come up behind us." At the point they thought they would be able to see who was trailing them, "it would cut off to the right or left, go round us, fade off, and then we would hear it coming again. This went on for ten or fifteen minutes."

The five soldiers made a plan for revealing the wily follower. Two of them, Sgt. W and Pvt. P, remained still, while the other three moved forward slowly. The other team would then move out. To their amazement, this triggered a complex maneuver by their swamp watcher.

While on maneuvers in the woods of Fort Stewart, the gunner on a Bradley Fighting Vehicle observed a Bigfoot through his night vision device.

"The thing started weaving in and out of the two groups like in a figure-8," Sgt. RB reported, and then none of them could hear it. When the soldiers united several hundred yards later, the following group reported the same pattern, "that it came between the two groups, around them, toward us, like it knew exactly where we were even though we couldn't see it."

When the opposing force was 400 meters (about 1,300 feet) distant, the five men established a patrol base and split into two groups. The first team, with Sgt. RB and Sgt. H, went out for several hours, and upon their return, two of the others would set out on patrol.

The first team advanced 200 meters (about 650 feet) and "heard something following us again." The men got to a more open area and "laid down facing the direction of the noises."

With no one to track, the skulker apparently became frustrated. After five minutes, "all of a sudden this scream-roar" came out of the darkness. "We looked at each other and said, 'What the hell was that?'" Neither had ever heard such a sound.

A minute later, "it screamed again and then we heard what sounded like a huge rotten tree falling and brush breaking." They heard a very large *something* running off, obviously on two legs, and the strange episode was concluded. It was 3 a.m. The soldiers had been stalked for four hours, and no one ever caught a glimpse of their follower.

"I knew that whatever it was, it didn't want us there, and it was intelligent," Sgt. RB related. Plus, from the roar, tree toppling, and stomping exit, it was obvious it had been a large animal. Sgt. RB and the others had been intimated by its' tactics, skill, and speed. The creature may have felt violated by human intrusion into its space. "If you wanted to go somewhere and never be seen, that would be the place," Sgt. RB stated.

From fear of ridicule, Sgt. RB told few about the experience, and found it difficult to describe even after seven years.

BFRO CASE # 17089

At 2 a.m. on November 12, 1998, Barry was the gunner on a Bradley Fighting Vehicle, an armed, armored tracked troop carrier that was maneuvering on dirt tank trails in the northeast portion of Fort Stewart, a swampy area featuring thick vegetation that grows to a height of ten to twelve feet. Barry was scanning for simulated targets through a thermal sight while the driver, his hatch secured, was driving with a night vision device, and the commander stood up in his open hatch using night vision monoculars.

When Barry entered a road intersection he would slew the turret to one side or the other to check for targets. At one intersection Barry looked to the right and the Bradley turned into that trail. As he scanned the track, he "observed something come out of the vegetation" fifty yards away, crossing from right to left and entering the brush on the opposite side. It crossed the fifteen- to twenty-foot-wide lane in three easy strides, not hurrying. The creature completely ignored the approaching Bradley, keeping its head and torso looking straight ahead.

Barry, who had long trained with night vision equipment, could distinguish clothing, hair, and equipment on humans, and estimate their height. This entity "appeared through the thermal sight to be one constant color from head to foot," which told him it wore no clothes. The being was also seven to eight feet tall.

Barry had watched documentaries and read books about Bigfoot as a kid, and he immediately thought this was one. Through the Bradley's internal communications system he reported the sighting, but the spooked commander ordered the driver to "punch it" and the vehicle quickly exited the area.

Barry's story was the primary topic of conservation at breakfast the following morning, with the soldier taking "some heavy ribbing over seeing Bigfoot." Later, another soldier approached and confided that his father, while stationed at Fort Stewart in the 1960s, had seen the same type of animal in that area.

BFRO investigator Stephen Willis spoke to Barry on December 24, 2006, and learned that the witness was then a police officer. Willis, a career military man, had observed a suspected Bigfoot during an expedition in northern California in 2006 and found it also "had a uniform heat signature" when seen through a thermal viewer.

FINDING BIGFOOT—DIDN'T

Finding Bigfoot is an Animal Planet series where four Sasquatch hunters travel around searching for evidence of Bigfoot. For Season 8, Episode 4, "A Few Good Squatchers," they decided to investigate Bigfoot at Fort Stewart, although to their disappointment the army refused to cooperate. The team considered the military reservation to be prime Bigfoot habitat.

The team did locate Luke Williamson, the Bradley gunner designated "Barry."

"I saw an object cross the road," he said into a TV camera. Startled, he knew immediately that it was Bigfoot. The two-legged, eight-foot-tall creature was only fifty yards away, man-shaped, and covered with hair.

The team also discovered others who had experienced Bigfoot near Fort Stewart.

In 2007, Bryan and his wife were riding a four-wheeler through the night along a railroad line. At one point, they pulled over and took a five-minute break. As they sat, a rain of debris-rocks, pieces of wood, or pine cones (they couldn't actually see the projectiles) rained down around them through the trees.

The couple also heard something walking through water too close for comfort. They cranked up and headed for home.

"I think he saw a Squatch," one team member declared. The four-person group was very positive regarding Bigfoot activity.

Jamie Wilkerson was just fifteen when she snuck out of her house one night to see her boyfriend. Late that evening he dropped her off at the lane leading to her home and she started a long, lonely walk down the avenue, brightly lit by a full moon. As she walked she heard something "that sounded very heavy" and was only ten feet away. Looking about, she saw what "looked like a big gorilla."

Jamie saw a clear silhouette of its shoulders. It appeared to be five feet tall and four feet wide, but was stooped forward, its knuckles resting on the ground.

The girl turned around and, grabbing the crucifix around her neck, prayed earnestly for God's protection. As she carefully walked away from the creature, she looked back and saw "its head was just following me," all the way to her house. "I knew it was something to get away from."

In the spring of 2006, Amy, who has two degrees in biology and has conducted field research, was driving down a highway on a bright day when she saw a "dark brown, very shaggy," creature cross the road in three large strides. After crossing the road, the animal stopped and turned to look at her.

Amy could tell it wasn't a man, as it was much larger than a person, seven feet tall and four feet broad, and was covered with fur. She was certain that she had "never seen anything like this before."

The frightened woman only wanted to keep driving away from the creature. With her heart pounding and her palms sweaty, she forced herself to keep her eyes forward and not look at the animal as she passed only several feet away.

Several times the Bigfoot hunters ventured into areas around Fort Stewart, where they whacked trees with a piece of wood (a prime bigfoot communication system) and one man, apparently the designated "Bigfoot Whisperer," alternated between making whoops and howls, hoping to lure a Bigfoot into responding. The researchers heard splashing among the abundant waterways and marshes and several wood knocks. These earnest Bigfoot hunters had no personal experiences to speak of but remained relentlessly optimistic about their quest.

BFRO CASE # 17089

During the summer of 2004, a soldier was leading his eight-man squad on maneuvers across a portion of Fort Stewart that was a wooded swamp on the edge of a plain. Dusk was near on a clear day as the squad leader emerged from the trees. The men first heard "a very low growl, then a high pitched scream." At a distance of 250 feet, the soldiers thought they saw an opposing force in the ongoing war game in which they were participating.

They called out twice to the opposition before they heard the growl again, and "it" stood up, which is when they "realized that it was not human." The lone figure was seven to eight feet in height, as estimated from the height of nearby trees, and covered with four-inch long matted, reddish hair. It moved on two legs and the arms, longer than those of a human, came to its knees.

At that point, the squad elected to conduct a strategic withdrawal, which the creature encouraged by throwing rocks at them. The animal then started loping toward the woods, 300 feet distant. Its slow jog was "twice the normal steps a man would take," and it covered the distance in twenty seconds.

That night in camp, which was surrounded by woods, the men continuously heard unusual sounds for five hours, including wood knocking, wood breaking, splashing water, and footsteps—first originating from one side of the camp, then shifting to the opposite side.

The squad leader described the initial sounds, which lasted half a minute, as a "very loud growl and scream unlike any animal I have ever heard before or since." The being's height and quick movements convinced the soldier that it had to have been a Bigfoot.

BFRO researcher Ken Johnston, an experienced Southeastern hunter, camper, and Bigfoot investigator, spoke extensively with the witness, who "spoke in great detail" of the encounter.

A member of the Georgia Outdoor Woods Forum referenced a report from my *Weird Georgia* website about Bigfoot sightings at Fort Stewart and others chimed in. One person knows several natives of the area who "were told stories of the EOD (Explosive Ordnance Disposal) Monster," also known as "a bigfoot, homeless woolly bugger or other creature" that lived in the Fort Stewart area. Another poster swore it was simply Special Forces "playing some mind games while training."

One man, whose father had owned property that became part of the reservation, wrote that a great-grandfather "wrote about losing chickens, pigs, cows, and strange noises late at night."

In an online posting, Guardian said he had grown up two miles from Fort Stewart and his father, born in 1911, had hunted throughout the grounds of the future base. His father was friends with a base commander at Fort Stewart,

"The CO stated that as an experiment the government had flown a male and female of every animal they could collect from all over the world and stocked the area with them to see how they would adapt. He also stated that experiments at the base were going on to enhance certain species."

Guardian said there were places on the military reservation where no soldier had ventured in forty years. Further, "knowing the government the way I do, there is no telling what else may be there."

Hunter Army Airfield

Hunter started life in 1929 as the Savannah airport. It entered military service during World War II, and currently hosts the air wing of Fort Stewart, allowing the 3rd Infantry Division to deploy rapidly, as it did for the 24th Infantry Division during Desert Storm in 1990. The facility has an 11,375-foot-long runway and 350 acres for parking aircraft. There are approximately 5,000 military personnel.

By September 8, 1973, an unprecedented wave of UFO sightings had inundated Georgia (which I explain in detail in *Weird Georgia*). Early that morning, two military policemen (MPs), Specialist 4 Bart J. Burns and Specialist 4 Randy Shade, were patrolling the perimeter road near Cobra Hall. At 2:30 a.m. they spotted an object in the sky with "quickly flashing lights." This unknown was "traveling at a high rate of speed from east to west about 2,000 feet above ground level," stated their report, filed soon after the experience occurred.

The intrigued MPs continued their rounds. About ten minutes later, near the 702nd Radar Squadron building, an ammunition storage area, and the base golf course, apparently the same UFO "came in at treetop level and made a dive," Burns's report read. This time the object narrowly missed the blue lights on top of their vehicle. The offensive maneuver made the soldiers duck, and the patrol car veered off the road and ran into a ditch. At the same time, in Savannah, Chatham County police officers saw a UFO dive toward the base.

The MPs were stuck in the ditch. It took them fifteen minutes to extricate their car, a frightening time as the UFO hovered 200 yards in front of them, its blue, white, and amber lights "flashing brilliantly." Back on the road, they drove to headquarters, with the threatening aircraft pacing them from a distance of fifty to one hundred feet. When Burns and Shade neared their office, the UFO flew away.

At that time, the Pentagon had "no normal channels for a communication of this type," reported Lieutenant David Anderson, the Hunter-Fort Stewart public information officer. Receiving word of the aggressive UFO, he directed the MPs to use the form for reporting accidents.

At 1:40 a.m., half an hour before the MP incident, Marcus Holland, executive sports editor of the *Savannah News-Press*, was on Interstate-16 at Lynes Parkway when he spotted a UFO sporting red, green, and white lights race across the sky. He thought it resembled a baseball and was larger than a star.

"I was traveling at seventy miles per hour and it outran my car like it was tied to a post," Holland wrote. The UFO circled the city, lights blinking off and on. After the newsman exited the highway to chase the object, it flew across Hunter.

"I called the county police when I got home and they said they had five cars watching it," he reported.

In Meldrim, Mrs. Miriam Tolver and her daughter, Davey, were startled by a loud "thud" that rocked their house for a minute. Running outside to investigate, they saw a large, brown-colored UFO that hovered 200 feet away from them. A single large orange searchlight was mounted on top, circled by smaller blue lights and even smaller orange lights. The craft was observed for three minutes, first moving west before circling back to Savanah.

When Corporal John Kitchell, from the Savannah Police Department, investigated a UFO report several hours later, he observed a large circular craft with "a large spotlight which changed color from red (to) green," with smaller blue flashing lights.

Meanwhile, back at Hunter Army Airfield, one of America's best UFO sightings devolved into bureaucratic nonsense. One of the MPs changed his initial report, denying that the patrol car had landed in the ditch. Next, the duty officer edited the document. Now the MPs had never left the road. An MP who had been open with the press and promised to reveal the "whole story," did not keep an appointment with a reporter. A day later, September 9, the MP said, "I'm afraid we aren't allowed to say anything." Higher authorities had told him not to discuss the incident. He referred reporters to the duty officer.

By this time, a "spokesman" admitted the "situation has changed" and he was "not at liberty to say" what that change was. He also was unable to reveal why the MPs had been ordered not to talk with the news media about their experience. Finally, late that day, Burns and Shade received permission to speak freely with the press, but they never did; they had both received three days leave and could not be reached.

Sometimes the story that arises after a UFO incident is stranger than the sighting itself.

MOODY AIR FORCE BASE

Moody Air Force Base, located nine miles northeast of Valdosta in southern Georgia, was established in 1941. During World War II it trained bomber pilots and interned POWs. For a time it was a Strategic Air Command fighter base. Moody is now configured for close air support (A-10s), combat search and rescue, humanitarian work, national security, and the global war on terrorism. President George W. Bush learned to fly here. The 9,300-acre facility has 6,200 military and civilian employees and 900 residents.

Ghosts

An odd Moody story was related by RICK9368 on October 29, 2009, via firefighterphotographer.blogspot. The account said that one night a call "was received by Moody Emergency services of a small brush fire on a road located on the backside of the base." A truck and two men were dispatched to the scene. After their investigation, they reported that there was no fire, only a very light fog, common in this swampy region. When the men radioed their findings to dispatch, they received an odd reply, spoken in an eerie voice, "Keep looking; you will find it."

Both men agreed that this was a strange response, and neither recognized the voice that had spoken. They radioed that they were returning to the firehouse.

Back at base, the men described the odd radio call they received at the scene. Dispatchers flatly denied knowledge of the message. The only responses they received from the firefighters were that they had arrived at the scene and that they were returning.

Firefighters and dispatchers were both adamant, so someone suggested replaying the audio tape of the exchange. The recording had captured the strange voice saying, "Keep looking; you will find it." No one at Emergency Services recognized the voice. Further, the dispatchers had not heard the statement when it was broadcast.

Later, the workers "were told that a security officer had committed suicide years ago on the stretch of the road in that same area."

The source of the words was never found, and neither could the call coming in that reported the fire.

"Could it have been him radioing back to the firefighters?" RICK9368 wrote.

DANCING WITH THE SPIRITS

As told to *Ghosts of America*, Dean was five years old when his family lived on base in 1989. One evening, around midnight, he lay in bed with his bedroom window open and a light breeze blowing the curtains into the air. Abruptly, two figures, an elegantly dressed man and woman, "appeared from behind the curtain . . . the man turned, bowed to the woman; the woman took the man's hand and nodded. The two then proceeded to dance a waltz . . . around my room."

Dean was too terrified to scream, but he was able to run into his parents' bedroom and burrow beneath the covers. Neither parent stirred, and at length Dean peeked out to see if the gaily dancing couple had followed him, and "sure enough they were dancing around my parents' bed."

He buried his face in the covers. When he got the nerve to look again, the dancers had vanished.

UFOs

In late December 1978, "Landry" was stationed at Moody. One clear night about 9:30, he was shooting baskets about a quarter-mile outside of the front gate when he spotted an aerial object, "a dark (black) solid V (chevron-shaped) metallic object," less than forty feet above him. This was a solid craft, seventy feet long, with a row of lights on the body and rows of white colored lights (four to ten) on each wing. He saw no jet flame and heard no jet or turbine engines, but did detect a high-pitched sound that he still cannot describe. The craft came from the west and flew east.

The UFO moved majestically and slowly, ten miles an hour, passing directly above the witness, following the highway straight toward the base. It was almost on a collision course with five F-4 Phantom fighter-bombers that were making an approach to the landing strip, violating every standard of air safety. The UFO barely passed above the jets, missing them by perhaps ten yards. The jets continued with their landing as if they had not seen the intruding craft.

The witness was "disappointed by the passive non-reaction, or lack of reaction by the pilots of the F-4 fighter craft," but there is precedent in UFO history of mysterious objects being visible to some but not to others in the same location. Landry described the UFO's behavior as intelligent, arrogant, and powerful, and proposed that our government "is no longer in control of US airspace." He told no one of his sighting for fear of ridicule from other airmen and discipline from superiors. (This information originated with *The UFO Chronicles*.)

Alfred was stationed at Moody in the early 1970s, his job to train student pilots on flight simulators. One evening in 1973 he was making a night milk run for his family to the base convenience store. The sky was clear when he "observed an extremely fast-moving light about thirty degrees above the horizon moving roughly south to north from the air base."

Fascinated, he slowed to observe and saw the UFO abruptly shift direction, "thirty to forty degrees to the east." Seconds later the object had disappeared. "UFO was gone!" he wrote on The *V Factor Paranormal BlogSpot* on January 21, 2012. Within a minute he watched two chase planes take off, "in what appeared to be an attempt to intercept the UFO," which was a lost cause. The jet trainer planes were supersonic, but the UFO was "at least five times faster than the jets in pursuit."

He believes it was a UFO that raced "across the sky at an incredible rate of speed."

In April 2014, a case from South Georgia was MUFON's "Sighting of the Month": On November 19, 2013, two qualified observers, John and Dave, sighted a large UFO over Adel, which departed in the direction of Moody AFB.

One of the witnesses was an air force aircraft mechanic, while the other was an army aircraft mechanic with a background in military intelligence. Each had thirty-eight years of experience working with military planes.

They were together at 6:20 p.m., just after dark, when they spotted a large UFO at an altitude of 500 feet and with a speed of about fifteen mph. It was silent, with a wingspan larger than a C-5A cargo plane (223 feet).

The aircraft passed overhead so slowly that a detailed observation was made.

"I could almost make out what appeared to be seams in the material," John said, "but it was not shiny—more dull and like carbon fiber. The leading edge was rounded, and there was no tail."

He walked beneath it "trying to make out markings," but it was too dark and blended in with the sky "so good the only way to tell the outline was that it was blocking out the stars and what few clouds were there. The ends had a reddish/pink glow but, not strobes or rotating beacons," that might be found on a conventional airplane. "I could not make out a cockpit."

The men saw a small object, like a drone, flying on the left side of the UFO.

The craft banked to the southeast, as if making a very low approach to Moody, and they realized it was triangular, "like a big wing. The lights on the back were from left to right, and white, not strobes, but pulsing. Dave said, 'That's a tight formation,' then as it banked, he said, 'John, that's one single object.' I said, 'Yeah, I know, but damned if I know what.'"

From the description, it might have been a man-made aircraft making a stop at Moody.

According to an Air Intelligence Information Report dated August 5, 1952, on July 24, 1952 three UFOs were sighted near Lakeland by a serviceman stationed at Moody as a member of the Air Force Band.

The three UFOs, "at various altitudes and distances," attracted his attention because "of their odd flying characteristics," and "he made serious efforts to follow their courses and maneuvers."

BALL LIGHTNING

In 1952, a T-33 jet trainer with an instructor and a student pilot aboard was warned away from landing at Moody because of lightning from a thunderstorm. Redirected to Brookley Air Force Base in Mobile, Alabama, it started turning west at an altitude of 13,120 feet. The airplane suddenly collided with a "big orange ball of fire," taking the hit head-on in the nose. The craft was shaken so violently that the student thought it was a mid-air collision with another plane. The low-frequency radio compass, located in the nose, stopped functioning and the pilots had to rely on ground control radio to vector them to base. The ground crew found the radio compass melted, but after it was replaced, the jet flew normally. The ball lightning strike left no physical marks on the fuselage.

009

NAVAL SUBMARINE BASE

Kings Bay

In 1959, Kings Bay started life as an army facility, a military ocean terminal for the shipment of ammunition during emergencies. A 200-foot-wide channel was dredged through Cumberland Sound and a concrete and steel wharf measuring 2,000 feet in

It looks like a submarine is surfacing outside Naval Submarine Base Kings Bay, but it is merely the sail of an old submarine mounted on a mound of earth and cement.

length and eighty-seven feet in depth, with three parallel sets of railroad tracks so three ships could be simultaneously loaded, was constructed. There were forty-seven miles of track laid in the facility, and temporary ammo storage facilities were separated by earthen barriers.

The terminal was never used for military purposes, but in the mid-1970s, the US Navy withdrew its nuclear submarines from a Spanish base, and Kings Bay was selected as a new facility for up to ten Ohio class ballistic missile submarines, equipped with Trident missiles armed with nuclear warheads. Active since 1979, the ships are part of the US Second Fleet.

The 16,000-acre facility cost 1.3 billion dollars and has the world's largest covered dry dock—700 feet long, one hundred feet wide, and sixty-seven feet in depth.

The St. Marys Submarine Museum is located at 102 St. Marys Street in the town, not on base. Within are numerous displays, including a periscope and many submarine models.

UFOs

"I live near the nuclear subbase in south Georgia," a witness wrote on *ufocasebook. com*. "For over a month, the sky has been full of moving lights." The night before he posted, "several of them have come closer than I have ever seen them." He thought one might be a stealth aircraft, "but I don't know of anything we have that can hover like this! And for that length of time."

He claimed that the population was warned of "trials and tests with unmanned drones over our area, but this is not ours!" The witness concluded that what he observed was just like the "Phoenix lights," (a controversial UFO case from Arizona in 1997), but he emphasized that this was not a hoax.

The control room of a submarine, complete with a working periscope, is preserved at the St. Mary's Submarine Museum.

A more substantial sighting occurred in July 1976, when the submarine base was under construction. According to NUFORC, the witness was driving on I-95 southbound to Jacksonville, Florida, where he was an active duty sailor. He described the UFO as a "glowing/pulsing round ball of yellow light, turning yellow/orange when changing directions, then back to yellow. Approximate size was up to fifty feet in diameter. No sound."

It was 11:45 p.m., the sky clear and bright from a full moon, with a few distant, thin clouds. The UFO came into view toward King's Bay, east of the highway, perhaps a mile distant, and approached to within one hundred yards, hovering above a pine tree farm. It was "bright enough to establish a clear definition of the numbers of rows and size of trees," which gave him "a fairly accurate guesstimate of its size and location."

The witness slowed, then pulled off the interstate and "stared with disbelief" for several minutes, before rolling down his window to listen. Silence. By this time four or five cars behind him and half a dozen cars on the north bound lane had stopped, the "passengers watching the object." Perhaps thirty cars slowed to gawk, and he and another motorist left their cars for a closer look.

When the UFO "changed from pulsing yellow to solid yellow/orange and began a slow but steady rise out of the trees," the men returned to their cars and most of the motorists drove off, "at very high rates of speed."

After running back to his car, the witness continued to observe the object as it hovered over the trees and returned to pulsing yellow. Shortly, the UFO changed color and moved to a position about 250 feet above the tree farm. There was no sound and trees were not blown about or otherwise affected by a propulsion system.

The motorist followed the UFO for one minute before it shifted to yellow/orange, stopped, hovered, and "was no longer pulsing but was a consistent bright yellow." The object "returned to yellow/orange momentarily, then back to yellow, sped completely over the horizon . . . in less than two seconds. No sound, nothing—just gone. At a speed I had never seen or imagined."

The witness had always ridiculed people who claimed to have seen a UFO. He described his encounter to his work crew, "and of course received the appropriate amount of heckling." He told no one save his wife for thirty-five years, when he made the report.

On August 15, 2010, a man and two friends were camping on Cumberland Island. At 11 p.m., one was asleep when the others decided to walk along the beach. The island had no lights and the area was "almost absolutely dark" when they spied an object flying above them.

"The aircraft was a large black triangular craft with a light fixed on each 'point' of the triangle and one in the center."

It was traveling south, silent, and low and slow, which allowed for a thorough study. It reappeared forty-five minutes later passing over their camp. The witness said it was "unlike any aircraft openly known," but did allow that it could have been a secret project operating from a local military base.

010

ROBINS AIR FORCE BASE

Just prior to World War II, Wellston Junction in central Georgia was chosen as the site for a large army airfield. The facility grew enormously during the war, and has continued to be an important air force base. For twenty-five years, it was a major element in the Strategic Air Command (SAC), ready to nuke America's enemies worldwide. Today, it is one of three Air Force Materials Command centers, a worldwide manager for aircraft and missile parts, software, avionics, and accessories. With 25,000 civilian employees, Robins is Georgia's largest single industrial complex. Four thousand military personnel and their families live on base. Robins is the lifeblood of the city of Warner Robins, one of Georgia's largest communities.

Visitors must tour The Museum of Aviation at Robins, the second largest air force display in the country. It features eighty aircraft, including a B-52, B-29, B1-B, F-4, F-16, P-40, P-51, SR-71, C-141, MiG-17, six helicopters, including a Huey, and eight missiles, plus many fascinating exhibits in four hangar-sized buildings.

UFOs

Warner Robins is a relatively new community. As a result, it has little claim to ghost stories, but with a massive air force base and many qualified observers of the skies, the city has accumulated a significant number of substantial reports of the aerial phenomenon commonly called UFOs.

The modern age of UFOs began on June 24, 1947, when Kenneth Arnold, a pilot, spotted a group of unknown objects flying above the Cascade Mountains in the Pacific Northwest. These objects were shaped like disks, which instantly earned them the name "flying saucers." America was swept with "saucer" fever as the objects were soon reported from every corner of the nation.

UFOs have always kept a close eye on Robins Air Force Base, where fleets of giant B-52s were once stationed, ready to nuke the USSR. Museum of Aviation.

Georgia was spared UFOs until a year later, July 24, 1948, when airline pilot Clarence S. Chiles and co-pilot John B. Whitted were flying from Montgomery, Alabama, to Atlanta. It was 2:45 a.m. when the pilots saw, according to Chiles, "what appeared to be a tremendous jet of flame," a dull red glow which "approached with incredible swiftness."

"It flashed down and we veered to the left and it veered to its left, and passed us about 700 feet to our right and about 700 feet above us," Chiles said, "as if the pilot had seen us and wanted to avoid us. It pulled up with a tremendous burst of flame out of its rear and zoomed up into the clouds. Its prop-wash or jet-wash rocked our DC-9."

They described it as enormous, one hundred feet long, and thirty feet in diameter. Whitted saw a double row of six square windows. "You could see right through the windows and out the other side," he said. A light, "brilliant as a magnesium flare," shone out of the windows. The orange red jet flame measured up to forty feet in length, and the speed was 500 to 700 miles an hour. The UFO flew southwest, on a direct course toward Robins Air Force Base, a distance of 200 miles.

Walter G. Massey was twenty-three years old in 1948, a high school graduate who served in the Army Air Corps during World War II in Europe as an Aircraft Engine Mechanic. He left the service in March 1947 and started working at Robins in September. He was single and lived in Macon.

On the night of July 24, Massey had not been drinking and was a transient Maintenance Alert crew member from 2400 to 800, 12 p.m. until 8 a.m., standing fire guard on the number two engine of a C-47 that was soon to take off. Visibility was 10,000 feet; the wind blowing to the north at two mph.

Missiles once protected Georgia's large Strategic Air Command bases. Museum of Aviation.

At 1:50 Massey was facing north, the direction from which the UFO approached, but he did not notice it until the rocket was directly overhead. It was in view for twenty seconds and departed to the southwest.

"The first thing I saw was a stream of fire and I was undecided as to what it could be," Massey stated in the official investigation report of the incident, "but as it got overhead, it was a fairly clear outline and appeared to be a cylindrical object with a long stream of fire coming out of the tail end. I am sure it could not be a jet since I have witnessed" jets in night flight, he stated. It "looked like rocket propulsion rather than jet propulsion," and its speed "was much greater," as if "energized by rocket propulsion." During his World War II service in 1944 he had witnessed the night launch of a German V-rocket.

The object Massey observed was at approximately 3,000 feet and the flame was longer than the craft. There was also "a faint glow on the belly of the object—a phosphorescent glow" that illuminated the whole vehicle. There was no sound or odor from the craft.

Massey believed the object "was about the size of a B-29. It might have been a little longer in circumference. It was too large for a jet. It seemed to be a dark color and constructed of an unknown metallic type material."

He estimated its speed at 700 mph and believed it was "one of the fastest objects I have ever seen," faster than a V1 rocket and considerably larger.

Asked if he was familiar with shooting stars, or meteorites, Massey replied that he was, but noted that those objects fell while this phenomenon flew "straight and level" and faded from view due to distance rather than dropping out of sight. It was Massey's experience that meteorites were round and bell-shaped, while his UFO was definitely "long and cylindrical" and "trailing a blue flame."

Of the UFO seen by the pilots over Alabama, Massey said, "the description seemed to fit my impressions."

Weather records backed up Massey's description of conditions, and the control tower confirmed that no aircraft had been aloft at that time. The C-47 he was attached to took off at 2:50 a.m.

Massey talked to Flight Control about his sighting and the case was given to Air Defense Command the following morning. He was interviewed by District Commander Lieutenant Colonel Eugene L. Cropper, who considered him a "competent and qualified observer."

Our second substantial Warner Robins UFO case involved two veteran members of the United States Air Force, one of them an NCO, the other an officer.

Staff Sergeant Lovett G. Harrell retired early on the night of April 9, 1950. He slept well and rose early to report to his job at the base hospital. His sight was 20/20 and he had not been drinking. The morning sky was clear with no wind. Harrell was going in early to complete a report that was due when the normal work day commenced. He left his residence on Mulberry Street in a taxi. Upon reaching the hospital at 3:45 a.m., he paid off the driver and got out of the vehicle, when his attention was drawn to the south by "a flash of light that seemed to be an explosion in vicinity of the Post Laundry," his report stated. There was no sound of an explosion, nor was there any sign of smoke or falling debris.

Harrell then noticed "two red-colored lights" that he assumed was an aircraft at an altitude of 500–700 feet. The object become more distinct as it approached, and he "could not hear any motor or noise." The object passed directly "overhead where it resembled a top that kids have that spins from the handle being pushed down," he related. "The bottom of the object was sloped and a distinct ring around the middle. There was a red light that burned constantly around outer edge and a white light . . . was visible inside the red ring. The object seemed to come to a complete standstill and wobbled in doing so. After gaining speed, the object righted itself. It made a sharp right bank over the hospital and gradually banked back to the left where it reached the swamp area and disappeared out of sight by gaining altitude."

The glowing edge, described as a very bright red, like a neon advertising sign, was around the widest part of the object. The glow was steady and there was no fire or sparks like from a flare. When the UFO was overhead, Harrell saw that the bottom was about twenty-two inches in diameter and the diameter at the middle was twenty-five feet. After the sharp right turn, the UFO traveled one hundred feet, then turned to the left and accelerated, "almost instantaneous," the sergeant stated, quick and fast, like throwing a baseball. The sighting lasted four to five minutes. Harrell was left with the impression that "the object was undoubtedly controlled by someone, and that the movement was deliberate."

Captain Charles H. McMahon had disembarked from an airplane at the base immediately before the sighting. He had three alcoholic drinks the night before but did not believe he was impaired, and had slept for an hour and a half on the three-hour-long flight. Friends drove him to the hospital. He saw Harrell outside the hospital and asked if he could sleep on a vacant cot for a few hours before he reported for duty. Harrell responded by asking if McMahon had seen the flying saucer.

Looking skyward, McMahon, who was nearsighted but wore glasses which corrected his vision to 20/20, pointed and said, "Yes, there it goes, whatever it is," Harrell stated. McMahon described a red glowing object the size of a star that did not blink but did brighten and dim. He estimated the altitude at 12,000–15,000 feet and the shape of the object was elliptical, like "a child's elongated toy balloon." Its speed was that of a slow aircraft on a steady course that alternately hesitated and continued in flight. He observed the object for three minutes and realized "that it was not an ordinary aircraft," his report stated.

The investigation showed that no military or civilian aircraft were present in the area during the sighting.

The witness interviews were conducted by Major Paul Kubala, intelligence officer at the base, who believed that the incident was important enough to invite District Commander Cropper to participate in the interviews. Cropper did so and wrote his own report.

Our third Robins UFO case involved three base employees who separately witnessed the same unidentified flying object. As in the second incident, the interviews were conducted by Major Kubala. The facts here are taken from statements made by the witnesses.

At 6:24 p.m. on January 25, 1951, the weather was cool and clear, with visibility at ten miles. The sun was setting, but the sky was still blue.

The primary witness, Guy F. Farmer, who worked in the Instrument Branch at the base, was relaxing on his couch at the Zeigler Apartments (# 388C), when his son raced in shouting, "Daddy, there's an airplane on fire!"

Farmer ran outside, looked up at the sky, and saw what he first thought was a jet plane ablaze. He then realized that the object was hovering in the sky and "an enormous fire or light" was projected several feet above the craft. There was no smoke, sound, or smell, and observation proved that the light was a steady glow, "between a blue, white, and a red," the likes of which he had never observed before. The light was projected throughout the whole UFO. The oblong object, at 4,000–6,000 feet, was about 160 feet long and had a uniform thickness. The unidentified aerial craft was a dull black without any windows and was described as "a flattened orange, but not round."

The UFO proceeded to move in an odd fashion. This is what the witness thought most peculiar: "the way in which the light 'pointed' the movement of the object. The point of light would move, then the object would move, as though the object were attached to the point with strings. The point of the light would lean over, then the object would move until it was directly centered under the point, then both point and object would rise."

Farmer thought of the maneuver as the object gaining elevation through a series of "climbing steps," which consisted of four stages. The UFO stopped after each step and hovered.

The maneuvers brought it to an altitude of 8,000–10,000 feet after three minutes as it moved from the south to the northwest. At the higher altitude it seemed brighter. After hovering for thirty seconds, the point of light took on an angle of seventy degrees, followed by the object, and the UFO disappeared at "tremendous speed."

Farmer was described as a licensed pilot who had dusted crops across the South for two and a half years and accumulated 2,000 hours of flying time. His vision was 20/20, and he did not drink.

Intrigued by his experience, the man drove to Cochran Field (the Macon airport) and asked if anything unusual had been sighted. An employee said he had observed a streak of fire at sunset, unaccompanied by smoke or sound.

The second witness, Kelvin A. Rhodes, a repairman at the base, was inside his Zeigler apartment (# 388E) when his daughter ran in with a report of the strange object. His description of the UFO and its movements matched that of the first witness. Rhodes said the craft had taken off as if "some tremendous force" had propelled it, like "slapping something off a table."

The final witness interviewed, Dock L. Barry, also a resident of the Zeigler Apartments (# 388B), told a similar tale. He had been alerted by a son.

Included in the file was a statement by Major Robert C. Higgins, weather officer, who testified that a weather balloon released earlier that day could not have been sighted at the time the UFO appeared. The document also listed every type of military and civilian aircraft aloft at the time indicated.

All three of these files were declassified on December 4, 1975, and can be viewed at Project Blue Book Archives. http://bluebookarchive.org/download.aspx

On November 27, 2001, a witness saw six objects in the sky over Robins. Examined through binoculars, they were upside down "Vs," both large and small. One witness got up periodically to check on the UFOs. At 1:30 a.m. one had disappeared. At 3:30 two remained; at 6:22 just one. "This is not the first time I have seen strange things over the base," the witness informed NUFORC. "Sometimes the objects were long and oval-ish with orange lights on the undersides." At other times there were "some really weird-looking ones." The UFOs were primarily seen between late November and early June.

On October 23, 2007, at 6:50 p.m., a student was riding to school with a friend when they saw a "strange red light moving real fast," a sphere faster than an F-15 or F-16, at 1,000–2,500 feet. The student was familiar with the aircraft that operate from the base, but this was unique, "a single red light . . . with a red glow around it," which left "the clouds in a weird shape like smoke rings."

Bird Fall

Our final historic report of aerial phenomenon over Warner Robins had nothing to do with UFOs, but was still a unique incident.

Robins Air Force Base may have once expected nuclear bombs to fall on it, but certainly not the 50,000 birds that crashed from the sky in October 1954. Whatever had struck these birds was nondiscriminatory, for representatives of dozens of different species were identified. Birds have fallen in many different places across the world, but never in such quantity or variety.

Freakish weather systems hit the eastern US in 1954, with a lingering summer and a fall that was unusually hot and dry. On October 5–8, the first cold front from New England arrived in the Deep South, creating severe weather conditions. Temperatures plummeted, winds increased, and light rain fell. On those nights a low cloud cover caught up with flocks of migratory birds, forcing them to fly at altitudes of 800 feet or lower.

Unfortunately, the birds encountered three obstacles, the worst being ceilometers, which are intense, narrow beams of light used at airports to determine the cloud ceiling. Ceilometers produce what ornithologists call a "sky trap." Of twenty-six bird falls that October, fifteen were attributed to ceilometers. Birds, attracted to the light, were temporarily blinded or disoriented and flew into each other, low buildings, or the ground. At Robins, there were reports of "birds flying straight downward in the beam and bouncing off a concrete runway!" according to a study conducted by scientists at Mercer University. In eight cases birds encountered radio and television antennae at 200 to 1,062 feet, and in three instances tall buildings and high tension wires were responsible for bird deaths.

At Robins, "dead birds were strewn by the hundreds over the runways, taxi strips, grassy plots, and tops of buildings." Each of the 2,552 birds autopsied, all collected from the top of a single building, exhibited hemorrhages and broken bones.

On the night of October 5–6, in the Northeast, there were five bird kills, involving sixty-one species and 2,756 birds in New York and Pennsylvania; on October 6–7, in the Southern states of North Carolina and Tennessee, birds were killed at ten sites, with 4,478 birds of fifty-one species involved; and on October 7–8, again in the South, 99,340 birds of sixty-eight species died at eleven locations, primarily in Georgia, but also in Alabama and South Carolina.

That night at Robins an astonishing 50,000 birds, from fifty-three species, died. On this same night there were bird falls at seven other locations in Georgia: Atlanta, 600; Augusta, 200; Savannah, 289; Travis Field (Savannah), 2,000; Hunter Field (Savannah), 25,000; Turner Field (Albany), 101; and the Okefenokee Swamp, 900.

Ornithologists thoroughly investigated this unique occurrence, the largest recorded bird kill in history, involving 100,000 birds of eighty-eight species. Their conclusions were published in *The Auk* (October, 1954), a publication of the American Ornithological Union, Volume 74, Number 4, October, 1957, in an article titled "Analysis of Mass Bird Mortality in October 1954," authored by David W. Johnston and T. P. Haines. This unique situation at Robins over a half-century ago is often cited in scientific studies of bird deaths.

Ghosts

On March 3, 2001, a C-23 transport aircraft from the Florida National Guard, 171st Aviation Battalion, with a crew of three, left Fort Walton Beach for Virginia Beach, carrying eighteen members of a military construction and engineer crew. Over Unadilla, forty miles from Robins, it encountered a powerful storm with heavy rain, strong winds, and poor visibility. At 11 a.m., the airplane crashed and exploded in flames. The twenty-one people aboard died instantly.

The victims were taken to a hangar at Robins as part of the accident investigation. Since then, according to one online source, "there have been strange noises, cold spots, and some of the machines have turned on unexpectantly."

A man writing on *STRANGEUSA.COM*, who claimed to have helped prepare the hangar, wrote that, "in the early morning and late at night lights go on and off in the hangar, you always feel as though someone is walking around behind you. Some of the sheet metal machines run by themselves, even when no one is around."

AnonymousUser, who retired from the Georgia Air National Guard in 2010, claimed that odd events "happened prior to the hangar being a makeshift morgue." He alleged that workers constructing Building 2370 (Fuels Facility) "spoke of tools being moved and strange noises. Strange occurrences are still happening. Doors opening and closing, radios changing channels, footsteps . . . are still reported."

011

TURNER AIR FORCE BASE

In 1940, the Army Air Force approached the Albany Chamber of Commerce and expressed an interest in building a military airfield there, if the city would purchase the property. Albany saw an economic bonanza and complied, purchasing 4,900 acres four miles northeast of the city, leasing it to the army for one dollar a year.

In late March 1941, construction started on three concrete runways, taxi ways, a large parking apron, a control tower, and several hangars. Most of the buildings were speedily and cheaply constructed, primarily frame buildings with plywood. They were utilitarian and meant for short-term use.

Turner Air Force Base was initially home to a fleet of B-47 Stratojet bombers.
National Museum of the Mighty Eighth Air Force.

Turner Army Airfield was activated on August 12 with a number of satellite fields at Tifton, Cordele Vidalia, Smithville, and Leesburg. The facility trained pilots to operate two-engine planes, and a navigation school was quickly added. In addition to American airmen, Free French and Royal Air Force pilots also received training.

In April 1947, Turner hosted the Tactical Air Command's Ninth Air Force. Buildings were upgraded with concrete and brick as runways were expanded to accommodate jet aircraft.

In 1948, Turner Air Force Base received P-51D Mustangs and F-84 Thunderjets. In January 1950, it became a Strategic Air Command base for the Second Air Force, providing escort fighters for B-29 and B-50 Superfortresses. This unit deployed to England, then Japan for Korean War service. In 1957, F-100 Super Sabers arrived, which operated in Alaska and Europe.

In preparation for the arrival of B-52 Stratofortresses and their tankers, one 12,000-foot-long runway was constructed, with a parallel taxiway. The SAC assets were transferred in 1963.

In 1966, a phase-down of Turner started, and the following year it became Naval Air Station Albany, consisting of eleven squadrons of the Reconnaissance Attack Wing. Several squadrons were deployed for duty in Vietnam and suffered casualties.

The military installation was closed permanently in 1974 and returned to the City of Albany, which proceeded to seek buyers. They were fortunate in 1978 when Miller Brewing Company constructed an extensive brewery that obliterated the runways and ramps.

Much of the base remains, including hangars, guard shacks, and fencing with signs warning against photographing the air base.

UFOs

Under UFOs in the Fort Benning chapter we related one of Georgia's most important encounters: the air force pilot sighting between Moody Air Force Base in Valdosta and Fort Benning on the night of January 28, 1953. The UFO was first seen flying above Albany.

At 9:50 p.m., a radio operator called the air traffic controllers at the Turner tower and requested they look to the west and determine if an unidentified object was there. The men complied and reported a circular anomaly that shifted color from a glowing orange to white. It was located and the operators kept the UFO in sight for eight minutes, when it vanished.

During this period the tower radar was being worked on by two maintenance men. On request they activated the set and found three to four objects on the screen. One was stationary, but three were moving at 300 degrees and a distance of twenty-seven miles.

Sometime between May 1966 and January 1967, an unidentified witness informed *UFOEvidence* that he had been stationed at the base and had a dramatic sighting, which was summarized as "Base attacked by 7 UFOs; all runway lights go off."

The witness, part of the 822nd Medical Group, saw "brightly luminous" UFOs at a height of two to three miles, too distant to determine size and shape, but he believed they were round. He brought several of his co-workers outside to observe the sight. The apparent craft executed "6 or 7 acute changes of direction, all 7 in unison" and descended toward the flight line, a mile away.

As they watched "a brilliant blue/white light lit up the sky" where the UFOs were, "followed by the sound of an explosion" and "numerous other flashes of light." With this assault the flight line went dark.

The witness said the air force blamed the blackout on a snake that had slithered into a transformer.

On the following day the man reported the incident to his superior officer, who was not surprised. Her husband, a MAC pilot, said that for months each time he took off he would find "a UFO off one of his wingtips." She warned the man that if he repeated the story, "I will call you a liar."

The witness described the UFO to the colonel in charge of hospital administration, who was not surprised, saying that a local farm worker had been recently attacked by one.

When he made this report on June 28, 2012, the witness was sixty-four years old and said he had BS degrees in police administration and psychology. He lived in Tennessee and had worked for the Chattanooga Police Department and Tennessee Valley Authority.

As a child he had seen a silver, blimp-sized UFO, and while stationed in Puerto Rico three years after his Albany experience "witnessed a school bus-sized meteor flash overhead," forcing an airliner to take evasive action. The object "turned the sky a bright pinkish orange," so bright he could read by it. He could see across the Caribbean for thirty miles and watched the UFO fly that distance without falling into the sea. It was in sight for five seconds.

Ghosts

Ghost tales have sprouted about an old mental hospital, which was actually the base hospital and never served as a mental facility. Reportedly, ghosts have been seen wandering within the building and across the grounds. People have felt quickly moving but invisible entities passing close by them and cold spots and breezes. There were feelings of chest pressure and unease and the smell of blood. Visitors have been pushed and poked and unexplainable lights cruise the halls. Unfortunately, there have been no substantial or substantiated sightings reported.

012

A CRASHED ARMY HELICOPTER AND BIGFOOT

The mountain phase of the US Army Ranger Training School occurs in the Appalachian Mountains, on the heavily wooded slopes of the Chattahoochee National Forest. Rangers are instructed by the 5th Ranger Training Battalion at Camp Frank D. Merrill, located near Dahlonega. The training is intense and arduous, and occasionally soldiers die.

On September 15, 1985, seventy members of the Texas Army National Guard's 49th Armored Division were participating in four days of tactical training. The thirty pilots and crew and forty infantry portrayed the aggressors against soldiers in the Ranger school.

Some once thought a Bigfoot family attempted to feast on the remains of a crashed Cobra attack helicopter's crew. Fort Stewart.

One Cobra helicopter gunship was commanded by pilot 1st Lieutenant Kevin M. Cardwell, a twenty-three-year-old grocery store assistant manager from Round Rock, Texas, and co-pilot 1st Lieutenant Michael L. Pope, a twenty-seven-year-old construction worker from Killeen, Texas.

At 8:20 that Sunday morning their Cobra crashed into a mountain slope forty miles northeast of Gainesville and burst into flames. There had been no emergency broadcast, the sky had been clear, and there were no other aircraft in the area.

The Cobra was supposed to rendezvous with another helicopter, whose crew "saw the smoke in the trees and located the craft," said Major David Cottam, a spokesman. "The aircraft burned upon impact."

An investigative team from the US Army Safety Center, based in Fort Rucker, Alabama, and Colonel Herbert Purtle arrived to ascertain the cause of the crash. Investigators concluded that the crash had occurred because of "engine failure due to first stage turbine failure."

The weirdness started fifteen years later when David K, who claimed to have been one of the security squad at the site, sent a report to the Bigfoot Field Researchers Organization (BFRO).

In 1985, he was a military policeman stationed at Fort McPherson in Atlanta. After the crash, his six-man squad was helicoptered to Camp Merrill and boarded a military truck to the crash site, their job to relieve Rangers and stand guard.

They hiked a quarter-mile to the impact site, which measured one hundred by thirty feet, and was permeated by the smell of fuel and burned flesh. The men set up camp, started a fire, and settled down to rotate sleep and guard duty shifts.

Around 10 p.m., David K was awakened by "the most god-awful howl/scream you could imagine." He found other soldiers with their .45 pistols out and ready to fire. They looked like "they saw a ghost."

All the men were awake and alert by this time, when "another howl/scream" occurred only fifty feet away. The men doused their fire and spread out in a line. As they started for the downed helicopter, they "could hear metal being pulled, thrown, and moved around at the crash site and I kept looking for a light down there as I was moving," but he saw no evidence of intruders.

When they were thirty feet away, one man activated his flashlight, revealing "three creatures . . . there among the wreckage and they were not bears! The closest one (about ten feet away) was holding a piece of metal from the helicopter and stood on two legs at least 7½ feet tall, covered in hair except for the face, which looked like a chimp; the one behind him (fifteen feet away) was dragging part of the pilot's body from the wreckage—he was larger than the first one—however, it was stooped while dragging the body. My estimate was over eight feet tall with the same facial features. I only saw the third one briefly forty feet away as it was running."

One soldier fired, and the flashlight was dropped as all six men opened up, firing into the darkness until they paused to reload. Thoroughly rattled, the men remained alert, "locked and loaded," until sunup.

By daylight the MPs searched but found no evidence of their encounter: no bodies or blood trails. They were relieved at 8 a.m.

David K never revealed his identify and no other witnesses to the bizarre tale spoke up.

This reputed incident was controversial from the start, and on September 3, 2010, Patrick Caulkins wrote BFRO:

"I was B Co MP USAG at Ft. McPherson in 1985 and was on the mentioned crash security mission to Camp Merrill. Very little of the story I read on your page is based in reality."

The team volunteered for the duty, he stated; they were not assigned. After flying into Camp Merrill, they received a Ford cargo van and MREs (meals ready to eat), and parked yards from the crash site. Several of them "helped the ranger medic bag and carry the bodies to the ambulance."

Caulkins said most of the men stayed up all night and found the evening "*very* quiet, and we passed the time talking and eating MREs. Nothing was seen or heard all night and absolutely no weapons were discharged."

The following morning they returned the van to Camp Merrill, then drove back to Fort McPherson."

According to this account, filed by a responsible soldier, the bodies had been removed before darkness fell.

"The Georgia chopper crash story has been debunked," the BFRO site now states.

013

A CRASHED F-4 AND UFOS

On March 6, 1994, two RF-4C Phantom jet fighters of the 106th Reconnaissance Squadron, 117th Reconnaissance Wing of the Alabama National Guard, left Birmingham for routine, low level, high-speed training maneuvers over west-central Georgia. The F-4s had advanced electronics capable of jamming enemy radar and tracking and suppressing anti-aircraft weapons. One of the jets was commanded by Captain John R. McDaniel; his Weapons Systems Operator was Captain Tracy L. Gilbreath.

There were reports of UFO activity in the area when an F-4 Phantom jet exploded over west central Georgia, National Museum of the Mighty Eighth Air Force.

The men were over Heard County when the pilot suddenly shouted a warning, and "everything happened so instantaneously," Gilbreath said, that the abrupt emergency "blindsided" him. A loud "bang" was followed by a violent lurch to the left that threw both men violently against the left side of the plane. Gilbreath's head swelled inside his helmet, and his shoulder hurt more than a month later.

Then, "the aircraft just dug in and stopped," Gilbreath continued. "I've never been slammed into a wall that fast before." He considered the force "extraordinary."

Gilbreath instantly activated the plane ejection system, which would rocket both men out of the stricken plane. Gilbreath was ejected first; McDaniel would follow after a few seconds to ensure that their parachutes would not entangle.

Gilbreath escaped, but unfortunately McDaniel was still inside the craft when it exploded, the debris falling over an area of 1.2 miles.

The crew of the second jet were stunned by the sudden destruction of McDaniel's ship. That pilot had glanced away for a few seconds, "and all I saw was a huge orange fireball."

Gilbreath was rushed to the West Georgia Medical Center in LaGrange for treatment of his injuries.

The crash site was cordoned off by security details from Robins Air Force Base, Dobbins Air Force Base, and two Air National Guard units, one from Alabama, one from Georgia. Combat engineers and a UF-60 Blackhawk helicopter with medical personnel also responded.

A board of investigation was immediately convened to determine the cause of the tragic event. That examination determined that a bad weld in one of the plane's twin engines, which occurred during assembly, caused a high-pressure combustion chamber to fail. Debris was blown into a fuel tank, causing a powerful midair explosion.

The manufacturer disputed this conclusion, claiming that pilot McDaniel had "over-stressed" the plane, and "crew-induced maneuver" was responsible for the accident. However, the company settled out of court with McDaniel's widow and Gilbreath.

Enter the UFO experts. There was no proof of a UFO being involved in the crash, but some evidence indicated they were operating in the area during this period. Perhaps they were observing the military maneuvers.

John Thompson was an insurance agent and UFO investigator who lived in Liberty Hill, six miles from the crash site. From his home Thompson heard the first jet streak by and saw the second, "alarmingly low and fast." Moments later his son saw the explosion. The Thompson family observed a dense cloud of smoke in the distance.

Bill Thompson (no relation), a fireman, EMT, and former fire department lieutenant in Chicago, was in his cabinet shop near Potato Creek when he heard the jets, a common event in the region. He saw both aircraft at treetop level making an estimated speed of 500 mph.

He also spotted something else: a silver UFO described as an "aluminum cigar canister with a screw cap," half to one-third the size of the Phantoms. It was below treetop level, in advance of the jets and accelerating away. Moments later, he heard the aircraft explode.

Two brothers were said to have observed the explosion and a UFO in close proximity. Another UFO sighting occurred over neighboring Troup County.

John Thompson suspected that for some reason the air force incorrectly reported the course of the F-4s, because some witnesses who only heard the jets should have been able to see them, while some visual observers should have only heard the aircraft.

On February 2, precisely two weeks before the crash, John Thompson had gone upstairs at his home to check on his children when he witnessed "a bright stream of lights that looked like Christmas tree lights just sitting there, maybe a hundred feet off the ground."

The objects were white, green, red, and blue and all, or maybe only one, large central light, were revolving.

One time the UFO made a "lunge for our house," then resumed its former station, which he estimated was one to five miles distant. The aerial phenomenon had "gigantic proportions" and was "as big as a football field" or larger.

Two weeks after that encounter the entire Thompson family—John, his wife, and their three children—saw six white, round lights, each ten feet in diameter, fly extremely low and slow, perhaps five mph, over a cow pasture and through a forest in the direction of the F-4 crash.

The silent UFOs, only half a mile away, flew in a single file format, weaving "through trees to such an extent that it seemed inconceivable that they could maneuver as such!" They bobbed up and down at irregular intervals.

Near the end of the observation Thompson remembered his video camera, although it "kept shutting down." He had the "distinct impression . . . that the occupants of the UFO did not want him to film" them.

The camera was unable to focus on the distant lights in the dark sky and captured only an "out of focus revolving white light." After operating for a minute, the battery in the camcorder failed.

Thompson, his wife, and their three children watched the UFO for forty-five minutes before retiring to bed.

Two weeks before the aircraft accident, a Stockbridge UFO investigator observed a white, oblong UFO, similar to a cruise missile, fly through the clouds at Goat Rock Dam in nearby Harris County.

The 1980s saw hundreds of substantial UFO sightings in west-central Georgia, dubbed the Troup-Heard UFO Corridor. Once a UFO seemed to be pumping water from Potato Creek, and there was an alleged crash of a UFO and recovery by the US military. A number of alien abductions and appearances of various creatures inside homes occurred.

014

THE NUCLEAR MISSILE BASE AND UFOS

During the Cold War, Georgia had two Strategic Air Command (SAC) bases: Robins and Turner. If war had erupted in the late 1950s or early 1960s we expected the USSR to send fleets of bombers to destroy those facilities. To protect these vital assets, four Nike missile batteries—two to protect Robins, two to guard Turner—were constructed in 1960.

Each battery was equipped with twenty-four Nike Hercules missiles, each tipped with two or ten kiloton nuclear bombs which would be exploded in the atmosphere

Robins Air Force Base and Turner Air Force Base were once protected by four Nike missile batteries designed to swat attacking enemy bombers from the sky with nuclear warheads. The bases, like this one near Byron, closed in 1966.

to devastate attacking enemy formations. The missiles had a range of ninety miles, a speed of 2,700 mph, and an altitude of 150,000 feet. The rockets could be launched fifteen minutes after receiving a firing order.

The Nike batteries were rendered obsolete by the development of Intercontinental Ballistic Missiles (ICBMs). Deactivation of the bases began in 1966.

These facilities possessed considerable destructive power, and might have been an object of scrutiny for alien intelligences.

One of the Nike batteries was located near Byron in central Georgia.

In August 1968, Mike worked at Camp Benjamin Hawkins, a Boy Scout camp adjacent to the Byron Missile Base. One night, he and two other boys "spotted a craft in the night sky," he wrote *UFO-HUNTER.com* in July, 2007, thirty-five years after the incident

"Its shape was that of two bright silver/white saucers placed face to face with a row of clear lights around the center," resembling those of an airliner. The UFO hovered 300 feet directly overhead, "and seemed to place us in an electrical field, because for a brief time we could not move our bodies." The craft "produced a sound much like a very high-speed electrical motor, shrill and almost inaudible."

After three to five minutes, the UFO slowly moved southwest toward the Nike battery before "it banked slightly and disappeared in a split second."

A Personal Story

It was October of either 1966 or 1967, and I belonged to a Boy Scout troop in Centerville. We always had a fall camping trip, a perfect time for an outdoor adventure, with temperatures crisp in the morning and evening and mild during the day.

Launching pads for the Nike missiles were separated by large earthen berms like these at the former Byron facility.

It was the first night, and I and a number of other scouts sat around the campfire late into the night, discussing what interests thirteen- and fourteen-year-old boys—primarily thirteen- and fourteen-year-old girls.

In the distance we spotted a bright orange light, not quite as large as the moon, which was clearly visible in another part of the sky. The object was unidentified and flying, so we stared at it and speculated. After hanging motionless for a spell, our UFO started swinging back and forth, each sway bringing it closer to the ground until it disappeared behind the pine trees. Half a century later, the incident remains clear in my mind.

Perhaps the aliens *were* nervous about our casual deployment of such powerful weapons.

015

A NUCLEAR MYSTERY

Dr. Strangelove has cut a thermonuclear swath through the Peach State since the Manhattan Project unleashed unholy hell on the planet. In the 1950s, we regularly practiced dropping nuclear weapons on the Soviets and the Chinese, believing the real thing was possible at any moment.

On the night of February 5, 1958, US Air Force Major Howard Richardson signed a "temporary custodian receipt" for 47782, a Mark 15 nuclear device eleven feet in length and 7,600 pounds in weight, with an explosive power 100 times greater than the bomb dropped on Hiroshima. The exercise was "simulated," meaning the device lacked a plutonium trigger, rendering it incapable of exploding. Richardson and his crew took off from Homestead AFB in Florida for a "target" in Virginia and a return home. The B-47 Stratojet was fast for its time-capable of 600 knots.

Richardson was homeward bound around the Georgia-South Carolina line when his bomber was "bounced" by a squadron of F-86 fighters based at Charleston AFB.

"I had a radar malfunction," said Clarence Stewart, one of the fighter pilots, "and then let's just say we got together one cold mile over Sylvania, Georgia."

Stewart's left wing struck Richardson's right wing. Stewart punched out at 35,000 feet, where the temperature was fifty degrees below zero, and floated forty miles before landing in a swamp.

Richardson "felt a terrific jolt and a bright flash of light occurred off our right wing," he recalled. One of his engines was all but severed from the plane, and debris wrecked a fuel tank and caused other damage. Richardson, a bomber pilot during World War II and a veteran of the Berlin Air Lift, thought he could get the plane down safely, but the bomb had to go. If it broke loose on landing, "it would come forward through the crew compartment like a bullet through a gun barrel," he stated later.

Richardson jettisoned the bomb over Wassaw Sound, near the mouth of the Savannah River, and landed in Savannah at Hunter Air Force Base, barely stopping at the end of the runway even with the assistance of a deployed parachute.

"What he did was magnificent," Stewart recalled. The crew kissed the tarmac, and Richardson received a Distinguished Flying Cross. The bomber was scrapped.

Next morning, Lieutenant Commander Art Arseneault, of the Navy's Explosive Ordnance Disposal Unit 2 in Charleston, headed to Georgia with minesweepers, sonar, and a blimp. After searching without success for two months, the operation was canceled on April 16, the bomb declared "irretrievably lost."

Forty years later, retired air force colonel Derek Duke, himself the recipient of a DFC and four Air Medals, learned of this nuclear incident. Duke located Harris Parker, a Tybee Island seamen for over forty years. Together they studied the plane's flight path, tidal charts, and weather patterns to establish the bomb's location. Using a lobster boat, Geiger counter, and GPS unit, they believed they found the bomb in early 2004, ten miles off Tybee Island, between Tybee and Wassaw Island.

Military historian Doug Keeney was investigating every incident in which nuclear bombs were lost. In a box of recently declassified military documents he discovered a 1966 letter written by W. J. Howard, the Assistant Secretary of Defense, to a Congressional committee studying the same topic. Howard labeled the Wassaw Sound device a "complete" nuclear weapon, which meant it was equipped with a plutonium trigger.

Twenty-five capsules of plutonium were surrounded by 175 different detonators, and each had to fire simultaneously to instantly compress the plutonium to create a nuclear reaction. The Mark 15, one of 1,200 manufactured, was capable of incinerating everything within a five-mile radius and would create a 160-mile-long plume of fallout.

"Never in my air force career did I install a Mark 15 weapon without installing the plutonium capsule," said Howard H. Nixon, a retired crew chief who loaded nuclear bombs onto planes at Hunter in the late 1950s.

The air force maintained the weapon could not be detonated, despite the 400 pounds of conventional explosives and unrevealed amount of highly enriched uranium. The government believed it was safer to leave the bomb where it was, located beneath five to fifteen feet of silt. Removal would be expensive—costing up to $11 million—and dangerous, with a possibility of infecting the area's water supply with radioactivity. The greatest fear today is that terrorists might retrieve the bomb and use the uranium to construct a "dirty bomb" that could poison a city with radioactive elements.

"It's a nuclear bomb," stated Derek Duke. "It's like if I take the battery out of your car, then I try to convince you it's not a car."

"There is no doubt we've got a nuclear bomb right here in our neighborhood," stated resident Ken Wade.

On January 23, 2001, Sandia National Laboratories in Albuquerque, New Mexico, found little danger from explosion or radioactivity of the Wassaw Sound device. That is good, because in June 2005, after another extensive search, the Federal government again branded the nuke "irretrievably lost." The case is officially closed, again.

CONCLUSION

Military installations, whichever service they support, are based on the industry of war. Military personnel are all exposed to the same intense emotions, fear of death, injury, wounds, the unknown, and separation from loved ones, which only adds to the ordinary pressures experienced by people every day, particularly to the young, who constitute most military members and their families.

Unfortunately, we will always have conflicts to fight, fragile peace to enforce and maintain, and vital missions to carry out. America's young men and women will always leave loved ones behind to go in harm's way.

Military bases, with their endless angst, military secrets, and vast acreage, have led to many tales of ghosts, UFOs, and Bigfoot. We are not only haunted by ghosts of the past, we are constantly creating new stories.

"1982 Fort Benning Sightings." Terry, Georgia Bigfoot Society.

"A Few Good Squatchers." *Finding Bigfoot*, Season 7, Episode 5, airdate June 28, 2015.

"America's Lost H-Bomb" (DVD). Marabella Productions, 2007.

Baumalizer. "Haunted Fort Benning." *Your Ghost Stories*, October 26, 2011.

Bozeman, Senior Airman Christian. "Ghostly Encounters on Dobbins." 94th Airlift Wing Public Affairs, October 14, 2011.

Brooks, Peter. "My Scary Fort Benning Ghost Experience (YouTube). September 3, 2014.

Bulldog46. *Woody's Taxidermy Campfire Talk*. October 11, 2010.

Condon, Dr. Edward U. *Scientific Study of Unidentified Flying Objects*. New York: Bantam Books, 1969.

Darnell, Ken. "Former Soldier Relates Ft. Benning, Ga Incident." UFO Casebook, November 17, 2009.

Deannah. "Soldier's Home." *Your Ghost Stories*, May 19, 2009.

Desirae. "Bragg Cemetery right outside of Ft. Stewart, Georgia." *Haunted Hovel*. nd.

"Encounter by a squad on maneuvers while training at Fort Stewart." Bigfoot Field Researchers Organization, Report # 28526, Summer, 2004.

Ford, Wayne. "Tales of Bigfoot legend include sightings in Georgia—even Clarke County." *Athens Herald-Banner*, December 13, 2003.

"Fort Gordon GA." UFO-Hunter.com.

"Georgia chopper crash story has been debunked." Bigfoot Field Researchers Organization, Report # 2393, September 1985.

Gijoe_99. CastleofSpirits.com. nd.

"Guard Pilot Dies in West Georgia Jet Crash." *Atlanta Journal Constitution*, March 7, 1994.

"Interview with Bobby Garmon, W01 U.S. Army, Witness to Death by UFO." Interview by Paul Dale Roberts, February 12, 2013.

Johnson, David W., and T.P. Haines. "Analysis of Mass Bird Mortality in October 1954." *The Auk*. American Ornithological Union, Volume 74, Number 4. October, 1957.

Johnson, Eric. "Bigfoot in the CSRA." *Metro Spirit* (Augusta), June 16, 2010.

"Man approached at close range by man/ape creature at Fort Gordon, US Army Signal School." Bigfoot Field Researchers Organization, Report # 2218, December 1979.

"Man recalls a possible encounter as a teen at Fort Gordon." Bigfoot Field Researchers Organization, Report # 4236, June 1965.

Marietta Daily Journal, October 29, 1984.

Miles, Jim. *Weird Georgia*. Nashville, TN: Cumberland House Press, 2000.

"Night sighting through thermal viewer by soldier on Fort Stewart." Bigfoot Field Researchers Organization, Report # 17089, Fall 1998.

"Night time harassment of Army patrol on the west edge of Ft. Stewart, 5 miles NE of Glennville." Bigfoot Field Researchers Organization, Report # 4109, December 1995.

Offdutycop. "Fort Screven." Paranormalsoup.com, August 4, 2010.

Olepapajoe. "Fort Benning, Georgia." *Your Ghost Stories*, September 13, 2011.

Project Blue Book Archives (Robins Air Force Base, 1948). MAXW-PBB4; pages 119–124. Declassified December 4, 1975.

Project Blue Book Archives (Robins Air Force Base, 1950). NARA-PBB90; pages 378–388. Declassified December 4, 1975.

Project Blue Book Archives (Robins Air Force Base, 1951). NARA-PBB90; pages 972–979. Declassified December 4, 1975.

Rhondaskppr. "The Soldier." *Your Ghost Stories*, May 18, 2010.

RICK9368. "Ghost Encounter at Moody AFB?" Firefighterphotographer.blogspot. com, October 29, 2009.

Roberts, Paul Dale. "Another Witness for Incident at Fort Benning." Interview with Ocelot, August 12, 2015.

Roberts, Paul Dale. "The saga of CSM James Norton: Detained." April 9, 2011.

Ruppelt, Edward J. *The Report on Unidentified Flying Objects*. New York: Ace Books, 1956.

Savannah Morning News. September 9, 10, 1973.

Serafin, Faith. *Haunted Columbus, Georgia, Phantoms of the Fountain City*. Charleston, SC: The History Press, 2012.

"Serviceman Observes UFOs Over Moody Air Force Base Valdosta." *The V Factor Paranormal* Blogspot, January 27, 2012.

Soldier1. "Benning Haunted." *Your Ghost Stories*, November 17, 2009.

Stepp, Diane R. *Atlanta Journal Constitution*, October 31, 1985.

"Tests Fail to Detect Radiation in Search for Lost Nuke." *Savannah Morning News*, April 12, 2003.

Thompson, John C. "The Enigmatic Troup-Heard Corridor." MUFON, 1998.

Turner, Renee. "Two National Guard Pilots Die in Copter Crash." *Atlanta Journal Constitution*, September 16, 1985.

"UFO Sighting: Albany, Georgia, United States–1966." UFOevidence.com, June 28, 2012.

"UFO Sighting: Fort Stewart, Georgia, United States." UFOevidence.com, June 24, 2006.

"Underground Bases." MetaFilter.com, July 21, 2006.

Vasquez, John, and Bruce Stephen Holms. *Incident at Fort Benning*. Santa Barbara, CA: Timeless Voyager Press, 2000.

"Witness Recounts V-Shaped UFO near Moody Air Force Base." *MY UFO EXPERIENCE*, January 15, 2009.

JIM MILES is a retired educator who has written fourteen books: seven about the Civil War and seven about the paranormal in Georgia. The History Book Club has featured five of his books. He has worked on documentaries with both the History Channel and the Weather Channel. During a forty-five-year writing career, Jim has authored hundreds of articles and blogs about Georgia history, archaeology, and travel, including the state's military bases. Jim lives in Warner Robins, Georgia, with his wife, Earline. Together, they have driven tens of thousands of miles exploring their haunted state.